KEEP OUT OF THE
REACH OF PARENTS

KEEP OUT OF THE REACH OF PARENTS

A Teenager's Guide to Bringing Them Up

John Farman

Piccadilly Press · London

Phototypeset by Spooner Graphics, London NW5,
Printed and bound by WBC Limited, Bridgend, Mid Glamorgan,
for the publishers, Piccadilly Press Ltd.,
5 Castle Road, London NW1 8PR

A catalogue record for this book is available from the British
Library

ISBN   1-85340-118-8 (hardback)
        1-85340-113-7 (trade paperback)

John Farman is British and lives in South West London. He has an
MA (Design) from the Royal College of Art, and the lowest ever
recorded mark in Maths 'O' level. He has worked extensively in
advertising and publishing. Piccadilly Press also published his
best-selling books, *The Very Bloody History of Britain: Without the
Boring Bits* and *A Suspiciously Simple History of Science and
Invention: Without the Boring Bits.*

Introduction

INTRODUCTION

There have been far too many books written for parents on the subject of how to cope with their difficult teenagers. Some are not bad, some are a waste of time, but all of them have one thing in common: they dump the lion's share of any family feud on your shoulders. OK, we all know that teenagers, at some time or other, are selfish, sulky, unreasonable and often a real pain in the bum; but there are, and always have been, lots of reasons for them being that way.

If it isn't bad enough having to cope with all the physical and emotional changes, you're expected to work harder than you've ever had to before in order to pass a load of exams that you're told will affect the rest of your lives. Great!

And if all that isn't bad enough, your parents seem to suffer total amnesia when it comes to remembering what it was like when they were your age, a bit like forgetting to press the SAVE button on a computer. They lead you to believe they were like little angels from the planet PERFECT.

PARENTS KEEP OUT

This book is for you, the one having to deal with it all. I wrote it to help you cope with your often well meaning, but usually out of touch, parents. You might find that some of the chapters deal with the sort of issues that don't affect you. However, even if your mum and dad are psychologists specializing in adolescent behaviour (and we all know how often they get it wrong), or you're a right goody-goody and never put a foot (or anything else) out of place, you will be bound to face at least some of these issues which can make growing up a drag . . .

Chapter 1

HOME(WORK) AND AWAY
Coping with school and parents

The subject of homework is almost guaranteed to create a
cold war in the best of households. You can tell your
parents that you are doing what is required till you're blue
in the face, but they never quite believe you're telling the
truth. Here is the sort of stupid, non-productive chat a
daughter might well have with her father.

Father:
> *"Where exactly do you think you're going* (the old war-
> cry). *Have you finished that homework?"*

Teenager:
> *"Panic not, Dad. We've got a free period in the morning."*
> (Since when have they called a fifteen minute bus
> ride a free period?)

Father:

"When I was your age I realised the value of education. I . . ."

Teenager:

"You're not going to say you wouldn't be where you are today if you hadn't studied, are you?"

Father:

"Don't be flippant. You wait till you get out in the big world. Jobs aren't growing on trees my girl." (Unless you go into the world of fruit picking.)

Teenager:

"I hardly think that going round to Cathy's for half an hour is going to seriously affect the complete course of my life, Daddy dear." (Could be the right moment to blink charmingly and smile. Fathers are usually a pushover for this.)

Father:

"You've never been round there for only half an hour in your life. Don't blame me when you can't pass an exam or get a job. Okay, that's it, I'm not going to say all this again." (I think there's a faint chance that he just might.)

Teenager (under her breath):

"God, if only that were true. I spend more time arguing with him about homework than actually doing it."

FATHER'S VERSION

I really hate having to nag but it really is for her own good. I'm sure kids these days don't realise how tough it is out there. If I had my teenage years again I'd work twice as hard. All she seems to be interested in is clothes, boys, and her dreadful music. Fat lot of good they'll do her when sitting in front of an exam paper or struggling through her first interview.

DAUGHTER'S VERSION

He really should get a bloody Duke of Edinburgh Award
for persistence. I've heard all that do-as-I-did stuff so many
times. Anyway, what's all this fuss about a good job. For a
start there aren't any, and for a second, I'm not so sure I
even want one, if I'm going to end up as a boring old
grumbler like him. According to his all-knowingness, if I
fail a single GCSE, I'll be cast into eternal damnation
(probably with all those stupid books). I wish he'd stop
getting so steamed up over something that is, at the end of
the day, down to me. If only he'd leave me to it, I'm sure I'll
do better in my own way.

WHAT A DRAG

Unless you're a swot, homework is probably one of the
worst chores that you'll ever have to contend with. Let's
face it, if you study all day, it's a right drag to have to think
about it out of school as well. After all, why be reading
about biology, for instance, when you could be out doing
the fieldwork in the park (or field)?

It often seems that we get our education at exactly the
wrong time in our lives. There are always so many better,
more exciting things to do. Think of all the things you are
missing while stuck indoors with you nose wedged in
some boring old book.

The fact is, I'm sorry to report, if you don't do it now,
you'll find that there'll never be a time that's any more
convenient. Don't go thinking that one day all your
problems (like making head or tail of this crazy world) will
be over and that life will be just plain sailing. As one set of
problems and insecurities goes, new ones creep up when
you're not looking and take over. In a world where you
have to practically queue up for a job at McDonald's, any
qualification, even if it's a GCSE in joined-up writing, can't
do anything but good.

HOME(WORK) AND AWAY

What's difficult for most of us to comprehend is the different speeds at which people learn. Some clever semi-automatons can skim over something once, shut the book and recite it parrot-fashion . . . three years later! The rest of us have to peruse it twenty or more times and then, when required to regurgitate it, find out the parrot has just keeled over (no dead parrot jokes thank you!). If you are one of those, please, pleeease don't go thinking you're thick (you can't be, otherwise you wouldn't be reading this book for the highly intelligent).

If you want a good excuse for the fact that you're taking ages to take anything in, try thinking of your brain as so incredibly sponge-like that it tends to get filled up with millions of fascinating miscellanea. It's hardly your fault that there isn't any room for the sort of garbage they ask you in exams.

A CAUTIONARY TALE

I had a friend once (notice I said once) who was a right brainiac at school; trillions of O-levels, A-levels, scholarship-levels, bloody everything-levels. But could he understand jokes? Could he hell! Whenever you told one he'd laugh that sort of nervous laugh you only hear from someone who doesn't understand — but doesn't want anyone to know. If you went to, say, a James Bond film he'd always be leaning over, spraying popcorn, and asking if you knew what was going on.

What became of him? He got a brilliant job in the city, earned loads of the old folding stuff; lost the lot on a dodgy property deal; chucked it all in, and now? Would you believe it, he's a village postman somewhere in Wales. If you can get a moral out of that you're a better man than I am, Gunga Din.

QUALIFICATIONS?

There's such a huge fuss made over passing exams that a failure can put a mental blight on you, if you're a bit sensitive, for years and years. I've even heard of some silly parents actually betting on their teenager's results. As if the pressures aren't bad enough without some silly, misguided idiot increasing them. Qualifications are important, but they aren't the whole picture. Bear this in mind: many employers would much rather give a job to someone who was bright, street-wise, confident (but not cocky), and most of all, willing, than some dull college kid with no personality and a snotty attitude.

REASONS FOR DOING HOMEWORK

The above stuff about personality wasn't put in to let you off the hook, however. An education helps because:

1. Imagine how much better your chances would be if you had all the above attributes AND a good few school qualifications stuffed under your belt.

2. It's interesting, and a bit frightening, to note that when your mum and dad left school, there was no recession and they could, more or less, pick and choose what they wanted

to be — then go out and do it. Times have changed, as they'll no doubt tell you at the local job centre.

3. Further education gives you time to build up your confidence and grow up gracefully, without all the pressures of finding (and doing) a job.

4. Having a rounded education gives you just that bit of choice. The ability to learn something and spew it out in an interesting way will always separate the men from the boys and the women from the girls (and the dogs from the sheep).

5. Universities or colleges are usually fab; a brilliant two or three years of being responsible only for yourself. You will also find that going into one subject in depth can actually be highly stimulating.

6. If you want to have a flash motor, wear groovy clothes, go on glam holidays, pull really sexy partners etc. you need plenty of loot. In order to get loot you need good earning capacity. In order to achieve good earning capacity, you must stand out amongst the also-rans. Education, without a doubt, helps.

Wait a minute! I hear you cry. I thought you said that some of us find learning really difficult. Difficult — but not impossible. There are a few study methods that give even the scattiest of us a bit of a chance. Here are a few:

1. Try to work, as near as possible, in silence. Anything that can distract, will. (Guns and Roses, Primal Scream, for instance.)

2. Try creating a routine. Work half an hour; rest for five minutes, work another half hour etc. etc. Much better to concentrate in short bursts than to sit daydreaming for hours.

3. Take something to eat or drink up with you so that you won't be able to use them as an excuse to stop every five minutes.

4. Do as much of your homework as possible at school.

5. If you do a long intense stretch, reward yourself. This can either be a favourite food, telly programme or anything you feel you're being deprived of by studying.

6. If you have a long period of studying, break it down. Give yourself goals, i.e. Maths will take one half hour, English essay three-quarters of an hour, etc.

HOW TO HANDLE YOUR PARENTS

1. You really don't have a large area for manœuvre here. The problem is that they are definitely in the right. This is always a bummer. You, therefore, have to convince them that you're doing as much as is possible for you. Then do it!

2. If this doesn't work, keep asking them the sort of obscure question you're pretty sure they won't be able to answer. This should embarrass them so much that they'll soon get off your back.

3. Tell them that they're your exams, it's your life and getting their own personal knickers in a twist is not going to be very helpful. You might, however, have a bit of a problem if they're the type who push you for their own self-gratification.

4. If your mum and dad are born naggers, try to find out exactly what they expect of you, and tell them what you think you're capable of.

5. Show them your work on subjects that you're good at, and like (if there are any). Then they won't worry so much about the others.

6. Make a show of doing it, and going up to your room (even if you're not).

There are also, of course, those hideous parents who, never having achieved anything themselves, devote all their energies into making their kid a prodigy. We've all seen those poor little horrors pushed, prodded, pampered and squeezed — all in order to fulfil their over-ambitious parents' fantasies.

If you're one of those, and you're having a hard time, let them know in no uncertain terms (like going on strike) that if they want to put all their time and money into making you the very best at something, that's up to them but, at the end of the day, it's your life.

Chapter 2

TO BE OR NOT TO BE TIDY?
Learning to live with tidiness

Far be it from me to say whether tidiness is a virtue or not.
If you prefer to live in filth and squalor, it's up to you.
Trouble is, you might have a slight problem with your
parents, who for some reason don't usually see it that way:

Mother:

> *"Have you tidied your room yet, it looks like a black hole in there."*

Teenager:

> *"Ho-Ho! Very funny. Anyway, what's the big deal? You don't have to live in it. You should feel sorry for me."*

(Nice try. You've tossed back some guilt, but it rarely works.)

Mother:

> *"Sorry for you? I felt sorrier for the family of rats I saw moving out in disgust."*

Teenager:

> *"Oh don't go on. I know where everything is, that's the main thing."*

Mother:

> *"I went in the other day to get your dirty washing and spent four hours trying to find the way back to the door."*

(Good joke, but it's like walking the wrong way up an escalator.)

Teenager:

> *"Don't rabbit on. Promise I'll do it on Saturday."*

(Always put off today what you might not get round to doing tomorrow: old Chinese proverb.)

Mother:

> *"I'll believe it when I see it. Just wait till you've got a place of your own, you'll soon change when there's no-one to do it for you."* (Possible, but by no means certain.)

MOTHER'S VERSION

Why do I bother? Every time I tidy his room he tries even harder to turn it into a war zone. He's so lucky to have a room of his own. I used to dream of having my own room without having to put up with my sister, and I'm damned

11

sure if I had, I'd have kept it clean and tidy. Trouble is,
I do too much for those kids. They'd soon complain if
I went on strike.

YOUR VERSION
God, can't she shut up. If I had a quid for each time she
goes on about my room, I'd be able to afford a house of my
own. Why does it bug her so much? She doesn't have to
live in it. If she thinks it's that bloody appalling, she should
feel sorry for me. Anyway I don't go on about the rest of
the house. If they want to live in a cross between Habitat
and British Home Stores, it's all right by me, as long as they
get off my back. The trouble with grown-ups is that they
always want to push their putrid taste on others — namely
me. It's all such a load of garbage.

ONE DAY HE'LL UNDERSTAND TASTE

There hasn't been a lot of research on this, but it could well
be that tidiness or slobbiness is handed down from one of

your parents. I don't know an awful lot about genes but I'm pretty sure there must be one really scruffy one that causes many people to be happy in total chaos. Some could leave an earthquake looking immaculate, while others can walk into somewhere immaculate and cause one.

DIFFERENT STANDARDS

A good example of this is the time I followed a friend into her flat and was convinced she'd been burgled. Drawers pulled open; clothes and underwear strewn over the furniture and floor, magazines and newspapers, wildly out of date, lying exactly where they'd last been read; and a forlorn neglected Hoover, covered in dust, sitting sulkily in the corner. "Oh this is nothing," she cried cheerfully, "I tidied up this morning."

HOW TO HANDLE YOUR PARENTS

1. *COMPROMISE*, the magic word. When you think you're ready for a big attack. Whip quickly round your room to make it slightly less disgusting — sorry — interesting.

2. If you're a fully paid up slob, and don't even notice it, you can periodically use it to your advantage. If a slob does something considerate for his or her parents, something not considered 'his/her' chore like washing the car or vacuuming the stairs or the dog, the reaction is often quite startling. The trade-off value is immense.

"Well you did wash the car which was a real surprise, so okay, you can come home an hour later tonight."

This really isn't fair on the tidy kid who not only never gets praised, but generally gets a mouthful if his standards ever drop to anything less than perfect. (Like a kind of household version of the prodigal son story.)

13

3. Tell your parents that living in chaos is a sign of pure genius and creativity, and that many great people have lived like you do. If you can't think of any, make them up. In fact, you could choose someone that they greatly admire — that could prove quite a diversion.

4. Try to convince them that the tidiness of your room is something that is affecting them for no good reason. After all, providing they don't have to look at it, why should it cause them such grief. Parents must learn to shift the responsibility on to you for things that, at the end of the day, they cannot, and even should not, affect. It will make their lives so much easier (not to mention yours). Memorise those responsibility lines and try them out, they'll sound quite good.

14

Chapter 3

YOU ARE WHAT YOU WEAR. ARE YOU?
Why parents always hate your appearance

I bet you wish you had an increase in pocket money for every time your mum or dad made some naff comment about the way you look. If there were a set of instructions that went with parenthood, trying to make their offspring conform to their standards would be top of the list. Fathers and sons are often the most explosive and conversations often go like this:

Father:
   "Isn't it about time you got that hair cut? You look like something that just crawled out of a rats' nest."
Teenager:
   "There's nothing wrong with it. Anyway I quite like rats."

Father:
   "You could at least put a comb through it now and again. Mind you, God knows what would come rushing out if you did."
Teenager:
   "Have you finished, Dad? I was rather hoping to go out in the next few days."

(Nice one — but be careful, that's a bit on the cheeky side. Parents, as you've probably discovered, don't like being answered back.)

Father:
> *"That's enough of your sarcasm. Anyway you can't really be thinking of going out like that, you'll frighten the animals and children."* (Very droll, I bet you think.)

Teenager:
> *"Finished? I'll be off then."*

Father:
> *"And do those ridiculous plimsolls up* (he means trainers) — *You'd think with the amount they cost, you'd wear them properly."*

Teenager:
> *"Dad! Keep up. Nobody ties their laces these days."*

Father:
> *"Well don't blame me if you trip and break your neck."* (Such concern. It's almost touching.)

Teenager (under breath):
> *"Don't tempt me: it would be a relief."*

HIS VERSION

What the Dickens does he think he looks like? You scrimp and save to keep a nice home for him to live in, give him all the things you never had as a kid, and how does he reward you? By going out looking like Fagin's scruffy brother. We give him clothes money for Christmas and birthdays yet he chooses to wear the oldest, filthiest stuff he can find. God knows what the neighbours must make of it. They probably think we don't even care. Thank heavens it's only a silly phase.

YOUR VERSION

What a total prat. He'd have me dressed like a bloody librarian — nice sports jacket, trousers with creases in, a paisley cravat, and a nice short back and sides to set the whole look off. Talking of hair: just because his front and back bald patches are racing to meet each other in the middle, he has to have a go at mine. Next he'll be doing a Robert Robinson and pulling the remaining strands across the desert. One day I'm going to shave my head and run down the road stark naked. That really would give the poxy neighbours something to rabbit on about.

Why is it that the silly old parents only seem to see ME dressed the way I do? All my friends are into the same stuff. And what's all this patronising junk that they whisper loudly to their friends about it being a phase. God, if I hear them say that one more time, there'll be blood on the Laura Ashley curtains. They can't honestly believe that one day, out of the blue, I'm going to come downstairs wearing the sort of dreary junk they do. I reckon I'm always going to look like this, so they'd better get used to it.

OH NO, I'M NOT TOO WORRIED ABOUT OUR RODNEY. I'M SURE IT'S JUST A PHASE.

ONE WAY TRAFFIC

Isn't it amazing, parents believe they have a kind of divine right to rubbish the way you look. Imagine their surprise if you did it back to them:

Daughter:
> *"Mum, PLEASE! You're not really going out looking like that, are you? What if anyone sees you?"*

Mother:
> *"I can't think what you mean. Anyway, I thought I might just try the slightly younger look."*

Daughter:
> *"Younger look? You're like a cross between Barbara Windsor and a geriatric Page Three girl. Have you no shame?"*

Mother:
> *"I'd have thought you'd have liked it. It's much more 'with it'."*

Daughter:
> "Oh God Mum, nobody's said 'with it' for 30 years.
> I mean, pink lipstick and stretch Lycra."

Mother:
> "You're horrid. I just want to look like the girl your father
> married."

Daughter:
> "Blimey Mum, when did he get his eyesight back? I've
> heard of mutton dressed as lamb, but this is like Jimmy
> Saville trying to look like one of us."

You see, that conversation doesn't quite ring true. If you
talked like that to either of your parents you'd be out to a
foster home before you could even say double standard.

SO WHAT IS FASHION?
Ridiculous! That's what fashion is. But wonderful at the
same time. Clothes are the only way we can show the
public at large what we are (or who we'd like to be). What
else can look cool one year, and be as naff as wearing your
baseball cap back to front the next? Parents and their kids
are just as guilty as each other of missing the point. You get
well uptight when they have a go at what you're wearing
but, on the other hand, wet yourself when you see pictures
of them when they were your age. "C'mon, Dad, that could
never have been fashionable — you look so naff." But you
could well be wrong; what might look just plain stupid to
you could well have been the latest then. You might think
you'll be wearing DMs, shiny cycling shorts or nose
furniture forever, but I'll bet you your next pocket money,
that your kids (if you're daft enough to have any) will also
roll on the floor laughing when you get out the family
album in years to come.

YOU ARE WHAT YOU WEAR. ARE YOU?

WHY DO WE LOOK THE WAY WE LOOK?

Most major fashion movements come from the street and from people in their mid-teens to early twenties. If you are in any way cool, what you wear this Saturday night is something that you and your peer group have developed on your own. Nearly all the famous designers, whether they be in Paris, New York or Rome, watch what you and your contemporaries are wearing like hawks. They then fiddle around with the basic look, embellish it by using flash fabrics, stick on a ludicrous price tag, shove it in some self-important magazine like Vogue and claim that it's original.

Vivienne Westwood, last year's designer of the year, is often credited with giving rather painful birth to fashion movements like punk. Oh no she didn't. It gave birth to her. She, like so many others, looked out of her window, saw what was going down on the street, cleverly adapted it, named it *punk rock* and flogged her own versions in her shop on the King's Road.

Department store chains also trade on the fact that most teenagers want to copy the more way-out kids and their pop idols on telly. They, therefore, clone this look and put out a watered-down, more generally acceptable version which, if they've got it right, is then snapped up by the general public. Mind you, I think it's fair to say that as soon as a fashion is in the stores and available to everyone, it will usually be as past its sell-by date as last week's kippers in one season.

Although the last thing we want is to resemble our parents, we do like to look like our mates and just a little bit like our popular heroes. When boring people (or worse, your mum and dad) can easily get hold of a new fashion, it's time to move on. There's nothing much worse than an adult who wants to look like a teenager. If your dad now wears a purple and yellow shell suit and a baseball cap with a pair of huge Reeboks, you'll know exactly what I mean.

I THOUGHT SHE'D APPRECIATE TRENDY PARENTS!

NON-FASHION VICTIMS
It's interesting to note that there are some young people who never seem to be the least bit influenced by fashion. All they seem to want to do is emulate their parents. They look fourteen going on fifty. The aristocracy are often a good example of this strange syndrome. Still, live and let live. At least they're able to recognise each other at hunt balls and point-to-points.

LEADERS OF THE PACK
Having said all this, there are only very few of us who REALLY want to stand out in a crowd. There might even be one at your school. All they care about is attracting

attention and they are prepared to take the flak for it. These are the true fashion gurus (and victims). As soon as they realise their look is beginning to pop up everywhere they move on.

SEEN IT ALL BEFORE
Lastly it's more important to realise that, despite whatever they might tell you, your parents would probably have been exactly the same. Whether they were Hippies, Mods, Beatniks (my goodness they must be old), Punks or anything else, all they were doing was following a look that they felt most at home with. If you're really being given a hard time, just remember this: parents rarely approve of what you look like. If they do, it probably means you are doing something very wrong.

HOW TO HANDLE YOUR PARENTS

1. If there are articles of clothing that your mum and dad object to more than most, keep them round at your friend's house or carry them out in a carrier bag.

2. If any of your friends are less 'acceptable' than you, have them round to your house regularly. In comparison, you won't look so bad.

3. If you are a girl and want to wear your skirt shorter than your parents regard as decent, again: take it with you in a bag; or change round at a friend's house. Of course, you could always wear something in a stretch material which can go up and down like a fiddler's elbow.

4. Make-up's easy. If you want to be outrageous (whatever sex you are), do it outside the house.

5. Tattoos, ear-rings, nose-rings etc. are something that you must think about seriously. Tattoos, for instance, go in and out of fashion as much as Gary Glitter. I mean, just imagine being stuck with Mr. Glitter for the rest of our lives (having said that, we might be). The problem is, as you well know, that to have one removed practically involves hacking off the part of the body it's on. The average tattoo costs about twenty quid to put on and at least £2,000 to take off. Punks and skinheads in the seventies often had slogans and obscenities tattooed on their heads and necks — 'Cut Here', 'Hate', 'Kill' etc. I thought they looked pretty stupid; but not as stupid as they do now, in their late thirties pushing a trolley, with a nipper in it, round Sainsbury's. Nose-rings also look OK (if you like that sort of thing), but beware, some people have the equivalent of a third nostril halfway up the side of their nose, after a few years of wearing them.

What I'm saying is that if you really want to adorn your 'actual' body, try as much as possible not to do anything that will be permanent.

6. Make sure you are not dressing in a way that upsets your parents just because it does that. If they do get upset, it's their problem, but there really isn't a great deal of point in rubbing salt in the wounds.

7. Once again, try to let them see that the way that you look doesn't actually affect *their* everyday lives. If they are losing sleep over it, they must learn that, realistically, it has nothing to do with you.

If you dress too outrageously for school then it's you that must be prepared to take the flak. The last thing you must do if the headmaster (or mistress) gives you a hard time is to rush home to mummy and daddy and ask them to do something about it. Personal responsibility is what the teenage battle is all about. All you want is for your mum and dad to realise that.

Chapter 4

IF MUSIC BE THE FOOD OF LOVE
Why have it so bloody loud?

I dare say when young Beethoven had his mates round to listen to music, his mum and dad used to yell up the stairs telling him to put a sock in it. Teenage music has always been incomprehensible to parents. It's one of the reasons you like it so much, but it's also a source of constant guerrilla warfare. Ever heard this argument before?

Father (bursting into teenager's room):
"Turn that awful row down. Your mother and I can't hear the telly, and the dog's left home."
Teenager:
"Loud! Loud? *You think this is loud? I can hardly hear it."*

26

Father:

*"Surprise, surprise! Your ears are probably worn out,
especially having those little speakers stuck halfway down
them all the time you're out. I reckon one day children will
be born with them fitted."*

Teenager:

*"At least they wouldn't have to listen to their parents
going on at them twenty-four hours a day."*

Father:

*"Listen, it wouldn't be so bad if it was decent music with
tunes you could whistle . . . but this stuff."*

Teenager:

*"Father dear, if I'd known you were going to be listening,
I'd have put on some Cliff just for you. If you want to
whistle his tune, you're welcome."* (Now what exactly
does that mean?)

Father:

*"At least he can sing in tune, which is a damn sight more
than this shower. What do you call this rubbish?"*

Teenager:

*"This rubbish, if you really want to know, is called
'House' and it's absolutely where it's at if you're under a
hundred."*

Father:

"Well I don't like it at this house, so turn it down now!"

PARENT'S VERSION

The trouble is, when we criticise their music they think
we're being square and don't understand. Unfortunately
we understand only too well. This repetitive drivel they
play these days has got to be mindless. It's definitely the
worst row that anyone's managed to come up with to date.
You've only got to watch *Top of the Pops* — not a decent
number on it. Bring back the Beatles I say, they'd show

27

these half-wits a thing or two. As for the volume, it's just plain inconsiderate. Why should we all suffer that junk just because she can't listen to anything without blowing the windows out. The only consolation is that it's probably just yet another phase.

TEENAGER'S VERSION
Please God if I do get like them (if I ever reach that age), order down some nice serial killer to put a bullet in the back of my neck. Why do they think that the only decent music happened when they were young? If I hear one more time that the Beatles were the greatest band that has ever been, I'm going to torch what they laughingly call their record collection. The point is, I don't give a monkey's if they like my stuff or not, so why should they get so narked if I don't dig theirs.

LIVE AND LET LISTEN
Each generation must have something its parents disapprove of. It's almost an essential part of the teenage kit. Music usually fits that bill nicely. People who lived through the sixties and seventies as teenagers, believe that they invented good music.

There is, unfortunately, just a germ of truth in this, especially where rock music's concerned. After the war, the communication gap between your parents and theirs was undoubtedly one of the widest in recent history. They were the first generation to stand up to their parents and challenge just about everything they believed in.

The hippy movement in the late sixties, although it seems a bit of a joke now, did have a serious side to it. Kids no longer wanted to go and get blown away in stupid wars on behalf of a bunch of power-crazy, blinkered, self-seeking politicians: and that was why they put beads round their necks, grew their hair long and claimed to love everyone.

MAN, ISN'T IT GREAT THAT WE'VE BROKEN THE BOUNDS OF MIDDLE CLASS CONFORMITY?

The birth control pill liberated a whole generation of girls fed up with playing Russian roulette with their bodies. At last they could have sex without wearing a wedding ring, or having to rely on the boy to be careful.

Most of all, however, and almost as an expression of this new rebellion, it dawned on most teenagers, especially in this country, that the popular music that had gone before was crass and they yearned for a music of their own. Recorded music was not, however, that readily available, and anyway most people were too skint after the war to buy luxuries.

Your grandparents would have sat round their radiogram (if they had one) listening, at best, to rather naff popular classics or, at worst, to awful pop records by over-made-up, stiff-haired stars in big frocks like Eve Boswell or Alma Cogan. The songs of those days were usually indescribably banal, and if you heard them today you'd probably die laughing. Titles like *How much is that Doggy in the Window, Gilli-Gilli-Ossenfeffer-Catsenella-Bogan-by-the-sea, Twenty Tiny Fingers,* or *The Toothbrush Song* by performers like Max Bygraves and the Beverly Sisters were two-a-penny. To make matters worse, few people had such a thing as a record collection so they would play the same ten or so discs over and over again, much to the distress of their long-suffering kids — your parents.

ROCK AND ROLL

The big break came in the late fifties and early sixties when kids first heard Rock and Roll, the illegitimate child of a strange flirtation between the rather sad negro blues and a sort of up-tempo country rock-a-billy music. It was introduced to this country in its raw form by a band called Bill Haley and the Comets. *Rock Around The Clock* their first single, was everything that anyone under about eighteen had been waiting for (without really knowing). It rocked and rolled over the country much to the distress of the establishment who, at that time, controlled all radio and television. If you think you have it hard now, you should have seen what your parents had to put up with.

A flood of great discs kept pouring in from the States, however, from legends like Elvis Presley, Buddy Holly, the Everly Brothers and Little Richard. In England, rather pale imitators like Tommy Steele, Cliff Richard and Marty Wilde produced even paler imitations of this essentially American music, but it didn't matter — rock was born and everything that had gone before it was instantly fit only for museums.

Your parents' parents were horrified and questions were even asked in parliament as to whether this decadent new music should be banned. Many kids in the late fifties were actually forbidden to play this disgusting row in the house.

IF MUSIC BE THE FOOD OF LOVE

RADIO LUXEMBOURG

As the only access to any new music was from the wireless (as it was called) the only station you could tune into was Radio Luxembourg. Unfortunately by the time the signal got here it was so weak that, if you didn't have a good receiver, this tantalising mixture of fantastic music and, never heard before, advertisements would fade in and out all night.

Despite the popularity of offshore illegal pirate stations like Radio Caroline, Auntie BBC kept her head under the blanket for several years, refusing to accept, especially on the radio, that kids over say eleven and under sixteen were not children any more. Finally, in 1967, they gave in and Radio 1 was born. A year later Ed Stewart (Stewpot) revamped the abysmal long-running children's request programme, which was the legacy of the recently deceased (and mind-numbingly boring) Uncle Mac. At last kids didn't have to suffer a diet of daft discs like *The Runaway Train* and *Teddy Bears' Picnic*. Teenagers as a force to be reckoned with had finally broken into Broadcasting House.

SEX, DRUGS AND ROCK AND ROLL

When bands like the Stones, the Beatles, the Who and, from America, Velvet Underground came along with songs strongly linked with sex and drugs, many of your grandparents, bless their cotton socks, went through the roof and saw them, like the Pied Piper of Hamelin, leading their children to corruption and degradation. But your mum and dad's generation had got a foot in the door and weren't going to give up that easily. Music was to lead to a mini-revolution in which young people gained their own voice which helped them to stand up to their fuddy-duddy parents.

WHEN WILL THEY LEARN

What's amazing is that your mum and dad, who may well have been at the forefront of putting the word 'teenager' on everyone's lips, seem often to lay the same boring old trips on you as their parents had laid on them.

But revolutions are funny things. Society, if left to its own devices, usually drifts back to the same kind of conservatism that caused the revolution in the first place. Your parents will often find themselves saying and doing things that they swore blind they would never repeat if they ever had kids. Hence the constant war over music and noise, for example, will run and run as long as parents still think they know best.

HOW TO HANDLE YOUR PARENTS

1. One of the reasons that your parents' music wasn't as loud as yours was because their record players (sometimes called Dansettes) had such pathetic amplifiers and speakers. One solution to the noise problem, if you only like music that makes your brain rattle, is to use headphones that plug directly into your stereo or tape player. I'm sure if you haven't got any, a word in what's left of your parents' ears would have them rushing out to buy some tomorrow, especially if they thought there was a chance it might shut you up.

2. Delve around in their record collection. You might be surprised. Among all the boring old stuff like Dire Straits, James Taylor or Randy Crawford, there just might be some gems that have had big revivals. Stuff like Hendrix, Stevie Wonder, Steely Dan, Santana — and even Abba (though God and the Swedes know why). You'll be quite surprised at their reaction if you start making nice noises about the music they like.

3. If there is absolutely nothing nice to say about their taste in records, the best thing to do is take your music round to a friend's house and let *their* parents put up with it.

Chapter 5

UP ALL HOURS
When to be, or not to be, home

One of the major issues guaranteed to get most parents'
knickers in a twist is the time at which their darling little
fledgelings should come home to the nest after an evening
out. However well behaved you may be, your parents will
imagine, at some time or other, you are up to indescribable
depravity when out of their sight.

Don't go thinking this is something new. I bet even
Joseph and Mary used to wait up of an evening, wondering
what time that young scallywag Jesus would get back after
an evening out with his mates — and we all know what a
goody-goody he turned out to be!

YOU'D THINK SOMEONE WHO WAS
GOING TO SAVE THE WORLD
COULD AT LEAST STAY
OUT A BIT LATER

Whether it be a disco, a rave, an action-seeking stroll
down the high street, or a meeting of the local junior Morris

Dancers (heaven forbid), you may still get that old Nazi-type interrogation both before you make your exit and also when you get home. The argument often goes something like this. As girls usually get a harder time than boys I'll use one as my example.

Teenager:

> *"What time do I have to be in, Dad?"* (Girls always ask their fathers first . . . they're generally easier. The reverse is true for boys.)

Father:

> *"Not too late, darling. You'd better ask your mother."* (A typical buck-passing trick.)

Teenager:

> *"Mum, is it all right if I stay out till twelve? That's the time all my friends have been told, and Dad didn't seem to mind."* (Two white lies . . . 1. That everyone else has easy-going parents . . . 2. That the other parent has already said yes.)

Mother:

> *"No. I'd like you back for 11.00. It's quite late enough."* (Late enough for what? you ask yourselves.)

Teenager:

> *"Oh Mum! that's pathetic. I'll seem a right twit having to go before everyone else. Pleeease! Do I have to leave at eleven?"* (Clever, but slightly obvious, ploy to gain extra 'coming home' time.)

Mother:

> *"You're not leaving at eleven. That's when you'll be back here."* (Neatly cut off at the pass.)

Teenager:

> *"But Mum, there'll be no time for anything if I leave so early."* (Bad mistake. It leaves you wide open.)

Mother:

> *"So what do you want to do that involves being there another hour?"*

Teenager:

> *"How do I know? — It's a party."*

Mother:

> *"What sort of a party?"*

Teenager:

> *"Oh, you know — pass the parcel, jelly and ice cream, a conjuror, balloons outside the front door . . . "* (Sarcasm seldom works. Be careful.)

Mother:

> *"There's no need for that, my girl."* (Notice 'my girl'. Unfortunately, as the old saying goes — possession is nine-tenths of the law.)

Teenager:

> *"Oh Mum. Please let me stay till twelve."*

Mother:

> *"No! And that's my final word on the subject."*

Daughter:
    "But why?"
Mother (and here comes the most predictable cop-out reply of the lot):
    "Because I say so."

PARENT'S VIEW
Who would ever have thought I'd have heard myself saying stuff like that — a real blast from the past. I remember how wild I was when my Mum and Dad said the same thing. It's different now though, there's so much more out there to worry about. The worst thing is that I still remember all the dreadful roads that I could have gone down. It just happens that I had a great sense of self-preservation. Thank God, otherwise I could have got myself pregnant that time with that horrid Brian Perkins.

    The trouble is, I'm not so sure that our daughter has got the same degree of common sense. Why doesn't she realise that, if we do seem to be always going on at her, it is for her own good. If we didn't say a time to be back, she'd stay out all night, and we all know what that would lead to. Boys are only after one thing and always have been. I can remember them at school on Monday mornings, boasting about how far they'd got with girls over the weekend. I mean, look at her father, he tried to get me into bed on the second night, when his parents went away to Bognor. On top of all that, we didn't have AIDS to worry about.

DAUGHTER'S VIEW
Talk about out of touch. What's all the panic about? What's so special about eleven o'clock anyway? I feel like Cinder-bloody-rella. The only difference is that she reckons I'm going to drop my knickers on the stroke of eleven, or suddenly transmute into a dope-crazed, drunken drop-out.

Honestly, if I really wanted to sleep around, or drink myself senseless, I could do it anytime, and practically anywhere (and with anyone!).

They make out they were such little angels when they were my age. I bet they were even worse than us. We've all heard about 'free love' in the 'swinging sixties', and they didn't have AIDS hanging over their heads.

Surely, if they came through their teenage years OK, why shouldn't I? I just wish they could trust me.

PARENTS ARE ALWAYS RIGHT

So there we have it. The most common source of disagreement between teenagers and their parents in the world. Translatable into every language known to man. For you . . . naked, unreasonable, I'm-bigger-than-you authority. For your parents — the only way they know how to protect their beloved little darlings from the evertightening grip of the horrid world outside.

HOW TO HANDLE YOUR PARENTS

Ever been fishing? Probably not. There might, however, be something to learn by watching a good angler landing a fish. The last thing you must do, when you've got the thing on your hook, is to try and yank it out quickly. The secret is to play it patiently and gently. Let it think it's in control and then, when you've eased it over to the shore, slip the net under it.

It's the same with parents. Take it very easy. Here's a few handy hints:

1. The first couple of times you want to stay out late, act the dutiful daughter (or son). When the old dears say a time to be home, accept it and come back bang on the dot.

2. When you come in from whatever you were doing, volunteer bits about what you've been up to that evening (delicately censored, of course). The more you tell them, the more secure they'll feel.

3. Introduce at least one of the people you're going out to play with. Choose the most sensible, normal looking one (as opposed to someone covered in tattoos with rings in just about everything it's possible to put rings into).

DOES IT SPEAK?

4. If you plan to look outrageous, or just plain sexy (whether you're a girl or a boy) do it when you are out of the house.

For some reason, the prettier you look when you're going out, the more your mum and dad seem to worry (especially if you're a bloke). I bet Julian Clary's mum and dad were just a little apprehensive when he went out.

If you do all these things for the first few times, they should soon realise that there's a fair chance that you won't be mainlining heroin next week, or making them grandparents in nine months' time. Best of Luck.

Chapter 6

LATE TO BED — LATER TO RISE
Parents v teenagers,
the longest game in the world

I wonder just how many arguments you've endured with your Mum and Dad. It often seems that everything you do is wrong in their eyes. Perhaps you weren't their kid after all. Maybe there was a mix-up at the hospital, and somewhere there are these great, progressive parents wishing that their teenager wasn't such a goody-goody. Not only do you seem to piss the old folk off when you are awake, but even when you're trying to get a bit of shut-eye.

Mother:

> *"Are you going into hibernation or something? It's 11 o'*
> *clock. How long are you going to stay in that bed?"* (As
> long as you're allowed, I expect.)

Teenager:

> *"Don't tell me you woke up just to make* that *joke.*
> *Where's the fire?"*

Mother:

> *"I'll give you fire. Why are you lying around on such a*
> *lovely day? It's disgusting!"*

Teenager:

> *"I am* having *a lovely day, thank you very much. What's*
> *there to get up for?"* (Nice reply. Could get you into a
> lot of chores though.)

Mother:

> *"That's not the point. Bed is for night-time. If you went to*
> *sleep earlier, you wouldn't feel the need to sleep all day."*

Teenager:

> *"I think I should be allowed to do what I like at weekends,*
> *it's bad enough having to get up in what seems like the*
> *middle of the night on weekdays."*

PARENT'S VERSION

It's like having a blasted cuckoo in the nest. The whole
house has to revolve round this little monster. When I was
her age, I had to get up at 8.00 on weekends and help my
parents around the house and garden. Everything I ask her
to do she turns her nose up at. I don't even think she'd
agree with me even if she thought I was right. This
generation reckon they can do as they damn well please. I
just don't know where we went wrong.

TEENAGER'S VERSION

It's worse than living in Colditz here. I bet even those German guards didn't come round to wake the prisoners up every five minutes. Why do parents think that the way they live is written in tablets of bloody stone for everyone to follow. If it's not one thing it's another. Eat *when* we eat. Eat *what* we eat. Sleep *when* we sleep. Like *what* we like. It's never-ending. I bet if I ran away they'd disapprove of where I was running to. It's so unfair.

Parents, as a rule, do seem to confuse their role in a teenager's life. For years they have encouraged their offspring through all its changes. They gurgle encouragingly as baby learns to walk, smile proudly when she says her first words, praise her when she draws her first picture, and even leap for joy when she pees in the

potty for the first time. When that same little angel transmutes into a teenager like you, however, all that goes straight out of the window. You might be going through just as many mental and physical changes, be just as out of control of your day-to-day emotions, but for some reason they seem to change their attitude and judge you on the same criteria as they judge themselves. They don't even realise that having a new body that's changing practically as you look, you're bound to be a bit clumsy and imprecise.

As for imposing their idea of a 'proper' lifestyle, they're more likely to make you go the other way just to flex your desire for some amount of independence.

I'm afraid the truth of the matter is that, because they are responsible for everything you do, they think it gives them certain rights of ownership. A kind of benign slavery. By continually sticking an oar into their youngster's life, albeit for the best of possible motives, the result is often counter-productive. You must be allowed to make as many of your own decisions as possible, even if you do cock things up occasionally. One only learns by trial and error. Parents who constantly impose personal rules, and go into deep sweat if their teenager doesn't abide by them, are simply making sticks to beat themselves with.

If they could just learn to shift the responsibility, life would generally be a lot simpler. A young person is more likely to be a sex-crazed, drug-addicted old-lady-basher if they've been under an unreasonable pressure.

Caring can be expressed in many more productive ways.

HOW TO HANDLE YOUR PARENTS

1. Point out all the things that you do handle responsibly, even if it's down to feeding your hamster, helping the old lady down the road, or resisting the temptations you do manage to resist (if there are any!).

MUMMY AND DADDY DON'T MIND WHAT I DO. AS LONG AS IT'S NOT SEX

2. Tell them that if they keep on telling you what to do, and how and when to do it, it actually works against your becoming a responsible human being. Get them simply to tell you what they want done, and then leave it up to you to do it. This requires some 'giving' on your part, but you'll be surprised how much better life will be if you take a bit of responsibility on yourself.

3. Tell them that although you're grateful for the things they do for you, they don't actually own you. Nobody ever has the right to remove freedom of action from another person.

Chapter 7

THE ROOT OF ALL EVIL
Money. Who needs it?

There's one thing you can be sure of in this life. However much money you have, it will never be quite enough. You will often find that the richest people in the world are not necessarily the happiest. This doesn't mean, on the other hand, that if you haven't got a bean, you should walk around with a stupid grin on your face thinking how fortunate you are.

Parents usually hate giving pocket money and, when they do, often seem to think they have a divine right to dictate how you spend it. I suppose they think that with all they have done, and still do, for you, it should make you content, not want any more.

Teenager:
> *"Mum, can I have a couple of quid till next week? We're all going out this evening and I'm broke."*

Parent:
> *"How can you be broke, you only had your pocket money two days ago. I just can't think what you spend it on. You've no idea of the value of money."*

Teenager:
> *"In which case why do you always say you don't know where your housekeeping money goes?"* (Nice try, but we can all guess the reply.)

Parent:

> *"That, my dear child, is different. None of that money is spent on myself. I can't think of the last time I . . . "*

(there now follows a long list of deprivations.)

Teenager:

> *"Oh come on, Mum. You spent more on those few drinks in that country pub on Sunday than you give me a week. Can't you remember being broke?"*

Parent:

> *"I'll say we were broke, we didn't have half the stuff you have these days. We used to have to make half a crown last each week* (whatever that was). *And there was no coming back for more. You're lucky, we used to dream of . . ."* (Oh no! You've really opened a Pandora's box now. All intelligent arguments are lost. You might just as well sit back and wait for her to talk herself out. Then just ask again. She'll probably be too exhausted to reply.)

PARENT'S VIEW

These kids today think that money grows on trees. I wouldn't mind if they spent their pocket money on sensible things, but for all I know they're buying cigarettes, booze and even drugs with it. I'm sure if I gave

48

week she'd still be out of pocket by Friday. (Try me! Try me! I hear you cry.)

TEENAGER'S VIEW
I can't think that getting through a fiver a week is exactly following Ivana Trump. Honestly, it's as if she'd never been in a shop before. Only last week she asked me if I ever bought drugs with my pocket money. I informed her that, unless they start selling dope at car boot sales, there's a severe chance that my meagre pittance wouldn't quite stretch that far, even if I wanted it to (which I wouldn't admit anyway). I wonder what their reaction would be if I started giving them advice on what they spent their money on. It's all so unfair.

MONEY AIN'T FUNNY
Unless you've got *Superparents* this issue will never be fully resolved. However much pocket money you get will never be enough for you, and however much they give you will always be too much for them. I think it must be something to do with actually parting with cash. The parents might give you more if they could give you it by credit card or even cheque. Cash is so immediate and instantly spendable. It makes them nervous.

HOW TO HANDLE YOUR PARENTS

1. Try to get hold of your own money. Not easy in this climate. Saturday jobs are few and far between and very often they appear to be slave labour. There are, however, a million other things you can do (legally, I must add) without having to work for some old skinflint. Anything from dog-walking, babysitting, car-washing to gardening. If there is anything that you can do that someone else can't be bothered to do, you're in with a chance — even in your own home. Use your imagination. Also it's a great training for later. If you can make some loot now, the experience will stand you in good stead for all those tricky times to come.

2. If you do manage to earn any of your own money, your parents have no right to tell you what to do with it, unless it's something that could harm you physically. If you want to spend the lot on sci-fi comics or daft T-shirts, it's up to you. Having cash that you have actually earned gives you a wonderful buzz, as it's probably the first thing that your mum and dad can't control.

3. With your first money, buy them a little present each. It's brilliant PR and, with a bit of luck, will make them feel guilty about their past behaviour. Don't worry, you'll never have to do it again. The shock of the experience will hover over them for ages.

4. If you are aware of your parents cutting back and having a rough time financially, try and trim your demands to a minimum, and let them know that you realise what they're going through. When times get easier, they will remember and should reward you accordingly.

Chapter 8

THE BAD THINGS OF LIFE
Smoking, drinking and taking drugs

Hang on to your seats ladies and gentlemen, we are now re-entering Doublestandardland. Practically everything parents tell you about these three subjects will be coloured by lashings of second-hand misinformation and some degree of "Don't do as I do, do as I say". If you try smoking or drinking the inevitable argument could go something like this:

Father:
   "So how long have you been smoking?"
Teenager:
   "Who me? I don't know what you mean."
Father:
   "Well someone must have been smoking in your clothes. They stink of smoke and look, you're leaving a trail of matches." (Get out of that if you can.)
Teenager:
   "Ah! Well! Er, yes, now I remember, I think I did try a cigarette recently."
Father:
   "You're crazy. No! Not crazy . . . deaf and blind! Haven't you heard or seen all the publicity telling you that smoking eventually kills you?"
Teenager:
   "Well they don't appear to have finished you off."

Father:
>   *"Of course not — I had the good sense to stop."* (Can you guess where this is going?)

Teenager:
>   *"Ok then, I'll chuck it in when I reach the age that you reached, then I'll still be all right."* (Game, set and matches?)

PARENT'S VIEW

Why, oh why can't he, just this once, take my word for it. I admitted I once smoked, because I thought it would help. I told him I gave up because of the risks, but even that doesn't penetrate his thick skull. If he beats us on this one, next it will be strong drink, followed by drugs. We might as well give up now.

TEENAGER'S VIEW

Good Lord. Anybody would think I was on eighty a day the way he goes on. Honestly, a fag behind the shops on the way home from school is hardly going to have me in intensive care. Parents lose their cool so quickly. Every time

THE BAD THINGS OF LIFE

I have a half of shandy, they have visions of me ending up living in a cardboard box at Waterloo station; as for drugs, I'm sure they think that all the major world drug syndicates are waiting at our school gates. Why can't they just trust me. I don't want to be a chain smoking, boozed-up, dopehead any more than they do. If they keep this up they'll actually drive me to it.

SOBERING THOUGHTS

There's no instant answer to this; only parents who have never touched a ciggy or sniffed a cork can wave the flag of self-righteousness. Very often reformed alcoholics or ex-smokers are the strictest. This, of course, is rather unfair. Just because they went over the top doesn't mean that their youngsters are going to. Mind you, statistics say that if your parents are alcoholics you are four times more likely to be one yourself — Cheers!

Having said all that, if your parents beseech (or even bribe) you not to, you should really listen. Smoking is without doubt an addiction that is incredibly difficult to kick, especially if you start in your teens.

BE WARNED

To make things worse, despite their evil reputation, kids still think it's cool and grown-up to smoke and drink. Boy, you sure know you're grown up when your liver resembles a soggy beer mat or you are about to inhabit a nice, silk-lined wooden box courtesy of some poxy tobacco company. Most doctors will tell you that the one thing their patients consistently tell porkies about is how much they smoke or drink.

> *"Oh no doctor, you could never really call me a drinker.*
> *Just the odd gin and tonic to be sociable."*

The trouble is that many people are far too sociable . . . far too often!

So what chance do you, the average teenager, have? Well it's no surprise that 28% of teenagers between twelve and seventeen have had a drink. By the time they reach the legal age to consume alcohol it has been calculated that, on telly alone, a youngster will have seen alcoholic drinks consumed no less than 75,000 times (give or take the odd glug). Cigarettes, on the other hand, are seen less and less, except in all those wonderful old nicotine-stained films.

THE BAD THINGS OF LIFE

THE DREADED CIGARETTE

There will always be some paths that your mum and dad
pray that you won't follow, and smoking the evil tobacco is
one of them. It is interesting to note, however, that doctors
and psychologists have now proved that there is such a
thing as an addictive personality. This does not always
have to follow from parent to child, however, so don't use
them as an excuse if you already feel that you're becoming
hooked.

If your parents smoke, but forbid you to: try to
understand, and even feel sorry for them. When they were
your age, there were hardly any warnings against smoking,
as no one knew it was deadly. Cigarettes were advertised
everywhere and no one gave it a second thought. If they
still smoke it's usually because they haven't got the
strength to pack up. Most smokers loathe the habit and are
ashamed of themselves, wishing they could knock it on the
head. That's why a parent who smokes, and can't pack up,
is sometimes, strange as it may seem, more adamant than
the others that their kids don't start.

DRUGS

The society we live in today has a confused attitude on the
subject. There's never been a culture, since monkeys
decided to be men, that hasn't swallowed, sniffed or
smoked something to make itself jollier. Whether it be
dried grass, cactus juice or fermented snake's dribble, there
has always been something to drag us out of the drudgery
of being human, on a day-to-day basis. Nowadays, the
most common 'drugs' are the afore-mentioned alcohol and
tobacco, though most people are loth to admit it. But your
mum and dad's fears relate to the other sorts of drugs, and
their paranoia is often totally out of proportion to the real
danger. This is partly due to a fear of the unknown.

Many, if not most, parents have had some contact with them at some time. The kind of drugs that would have been around during their teenage years were marijuana and LSD. Heroin was there but wasn't as prevalent as it is now. And the more sophisticated and dangerous drugs like cocaine, crack and ecstasy came along a bit later.

COULD YOU BE AN ADDICT?

Again, it's the people who are addictive by nature who must be extra careful. The rest of us are quite self-protective, but at the same time rather curious. People like buzzes. If they didn't there wouldn't be fast cars, fairground rides, dangerous sports or stockings and suspenders. Drugs give you a buzz, but the kind of buzz you get varies enormously. Some drugs make you feel fab and confident, and others dreamy and highly intellectual.

The trouble is, like most things, the side-effects (like addiction) are often horrendous. I guarantee if cocaine suddenly got a clean bill of health, we'd all be sniffing it and smoking it while sitting as a family round the telly:

"After you with the coke, Jamie. Granny hasn't had any yet and you know how she loves to get high during Highway.*"*

Unfortunately some people become physically dependent very quickly, and some drugs are extremely user-friendly. Most parents know that a joint (marijuana) isn't any more harmful than alcohol or cigarettes; however, it is considered more harmful because of the fear that, having done it a few times, you might want a stronger sensation and start using stronger drugs. It would be naive to say that this never happens, and stories about kids from the very 'nicest' of homes, with brilliant futures, dying of overdoses or descending to the most ultimate degradations are not rare. Why them? Maybe because they're usually the only teenagers that can afford the heavy drugs. Drug addiction, it must be said, has no class prejudice.

The other problem with drugs in the nineties, is that a lot of the stuff around at raves or clubs is of dubious origin and composition. For instance, some of the so-called 'smart'

SOME DRUGS ARE OF DUBIOUS ORIGIN

drugs imported from the States were produced to treat senility and epilepsy. There have been practically no tests to determine the side-effects on able-bodied (and -minded) people. To be honest, the whole subject is a minefield. With a little care, however, you can pick your way through it without being zapped; but take great care, you could well become Mr or Miss Fuzzybrain at best, or Mr or Miss No-Brain-At-All at worst.

WHICH DRUGS ARE WHICH?

HEROIN *(smack, H, scag, shit, horse, blow)*
This is regarded as the big-bad-wolf of drugs. It was thought that because heroin was always mainlined (injected), this was the only way you could become addicted. (Let's face it, anyone who goes far enough to make themselves into a human pin-cushion must be quite a way down the road to never-never land.) Now, however, heroin is quite often smoked (called 'chasing the dragon') or even snorted up the nostrils in powder form.

Getting addicted is, strange as it may seem, not that easy. The 'rush', which is the end result, a sudden feeling of mindblowing, don't give a toss about anything, pleasure can only be reached after a few attempts. This lasts for a couple of minutes followed by a longish period of dreamy, drowsy contentment. Sounds brill doesn't it? The trouble is, as you take it, you build up a resistance and need more and more to achieve the elation (that you suddenly can't live without) which, by then, is not as great as it was. By this time the user is firmly on the track and entering a tunnel which comes out at the other end as total addiction and the dreaded withdrawal symptoms between 'hits'.

These aren't nearly so much fun, as the poor victim experiences a whole series of chills, bouts of throwing up, crippling cramps and unbearable itching. Without help at this stage, the next station (following the railway metaphor) is terminal.

As if all that wasn't bad enough, taking drugs by hypodermic needle has been a major contributor to the spread of AIDS. Drug addicts, being not the most together of folk, tend to share their needles. This might seem rather friendly, but if the donor has AIDS or is HIV-positive, the recipient will almost certainly get it too.

COCAINE *(coke, snow or charlie)*
Cocaine is far less messy. All you need is a drinking straw (or rolled-up banknote), a mirror, and something to chop it so it is fine enough to sniff through the straw, and loads and loads and loads of money. Coke gives you an even better 'rush' than heroin, and instead of making you all docile and pussy-cat-like, it makes you feel energetic, happy and capable of performing in front of thousands at Wembley Stadium. People on coke talk about the same old things, in the same old way, but *think* they're being brilliant, witty and desperately intelligent. It's known as the designer drug, possibly because it is mostly creative

people who use it, and firmly believe that it jiggles the old brain cells so that they come up with better ideas (which they don't).

The good news is that cocaine doesn't create an instant dependency, in other words it's not physically addictive. The bad news is that the crash you experience when all the fun is over, is so gloomy that you just can't rest before having some more. There are, therefore, a lot of once very rich, now very poor, creative chappies who walk around like zombies, with permanently runny noses (completely ruined by the razor-sharp crystals), swearing blind they're not addicted and borrowing money off all and sundry to support their 'non-habit'.

CRACK

If being broke and permanently out of your skull is not enough, there's always crack. This is basically cocaine mixed with bicarbonate of soda (just like Mummy uses), and water. When the water is boiled off, a white crystalline substance is left, which can be dissolved and injected, or, in a more purified form (freebase), smoked.

The 'rush' you get from this little devil gets you to never-never land real quick. The trouble is it only lasts for the blink of an eye, and the user, as if they've had an audience with God, can't wait to repeat the buzz. The net result is that you can be totally addicted after a couple of goes, and that ain't nice.

LSD *(acid)*

Ask your mum and dad. If they confess to having been hippies, then they will probably have taken acid or known people who have. If they don't confess to having been hippies, there are give-away clues, like your mother having a drawer full of cheap Indian jewellery and headbands, or

Dad having curious purple trousers with strangely flared bottoms stuffed into the back of his wardrobe.

D-lysergic acid diethylamide (LSD) is a liquid which is soaked into weeny bits of paper and sold as 'blotters', or in tiny little pills known as tabs. These give you hallucinations called 'trips', which can sometimes be wonderful — if you like swimming in fairy dust or having sex with a daffodil. On the other hand they can be horrid and like the worst nightmare, popping back anything up to a few weeks later. Some space cadets, bless them, thought they could fly on it and dived off high buildings. Unfortunately, they soon found out they couldn't. Acid might be non-addictive but it is said that some people who took a lot of it in the sixties have ended up with brains like candyfloss and the attention span of a none-too-bright goldfish. There is, however, little clinical evidence of this. It is, on the other hand, generally accepted that anyone with even the mildest psychological problem could get into severe trouble with acid, as it will almost certainly amplify the condition.

Modern versions of acid have colourful names like Californian Sunset and Purple OMS (fairly mild), or Strawberries and Bart Simpsons (fairly strong). If you wanted to do your brain in very quickly then Laughing Buddhas or Techno Splashes were made just for you.

UPPERS AND DOWNERS
Tranquillisers or 'tranks' which calm you down are called downers, and amphetamines, which wake you up and help you walk on the ceiling, are called uppers. Uppers are capsules or tablets and, in your parents' day, were known as purple hearts. They are now better known on the black market as 'dexies', 'blues' or 'black bombers'.

SPEED *(whizz)*
Methylamphetamine and amphetamine sulphate (poor man's cocaine), known also as speed, is usually sold in powder form to be dissolved in water and injected (ouch), sniffed, or simply swallowed. It was originally prescribed by doctors as a dietary aid, though I expect the only way it

worked was for the patients to get so out to lunch they forgot about eating it.

Cheap speed is sometimes cut (mixed) with Ajax or Vim to make it look as if there's more than there actually is. This is OK if you want really clean nostrils I suppose. At least that's better than another additive — strychnine (rat poison). Apparently the effect of strychnine is much the same as the speed, if you don't mind ending up like a dead rat.

DOWNERS *(Mandrax, Quaaludes, Tunol)*
These were all the rage in the sixties and seventies, but have now been largely superseded by barbiturates and benzodiazepines. These are known as barbies (what happened to Ken?) or bennies.

Overdoses are easy with this little batch of drugs, and you could easily become an ex-person, especially if you wash them down with alcohol. Brian Jones, the original lead guitarist and singer with the Rolling Stones, died when he took Quaaludes washed down with a rather nice red wine.

SOLVENTS *(glue, hairspray, nail varnish, paint stripper, lighter fuel, aerosols)*
These claim to give hours of pleasure to their sniffers with their instant ability to create excitement and weird hallucinations. They are legal and available at most corner shops for very little dosh.

However, there's always a negative side to everything. Solvents are no exception. The short-term side-effects are open sores round the mouth and nose (nice, eh!), memory 1 . . . loss, bad temper and skull-splitting headaches. Long-term are brain damage, liver or kidney failure, leukemia and a complete breakdown of the nervous system. A slightly longer-term side-effect is death, usually from asphyxiation or heart attacks. Jolly or what?

KETAMINE
A weird tranquilliser that, although it has been around for years, has now started turning up on the club scene. Believe it or not, this drug is usually used in the veterinary business for knocking out anything up to an elephant. Apparently it was even given to soldiers who'd unfortunately had their arms and legs blown off. It seems that after a shot of ketamine they didn't seem to mind that much. Having said that, the chances of losing your arms and legs at the average disco are thankfully rather remote. Also, it stands to reason that the numbing effect of this drug renders you practically non-operational. If you like the idea of having the drive and sex appeal of a dopey elephant, be my guest.

AMYL NITRATE *(poppas)*
This substance has been around for years and is, strangely enough, not illegal. It is relatively inexpensive and comes either in nice little phials or even by the bottle. Perfect, I hear you say! Ah, that's not quite true. Poppas, not only smell absolutely disgusting, but are capable of speeding the heart rate up so much, that it can give the jolly raver a heart attack. Back to the drawing board!

ECSTASY (Es, MDMA)

This is the drug that you are more than likely, at some time, to come across at a rave, disco or party. It is an amphetamine related somehow to the nutmeg and comes with many different names either in capsule or tablet form. It is known as a combination drug as it contains a mixture of different substances designed like a cocktail specifically for music and dancing. It gives you the energy and focus to leap around and buzz for hours on end, even though, to people who haven't taken it, you often appear and sound totally out to lunch. Ecstasy can be dangerous — not because of what it does to you physically — but more because of what you tend to do if you've taken it. All the major casualties have been caused by heat stroke and severe dehydration. If regular liquid (not alcohol) is not taken on board while dancing for hours on end, it stands to reason that something's bound to blow; a bit like running a car with no oil or water. We are only relatively simple machines after all (some simpler than others!).

JUST ADD WATER.

Also there's been a tendency for some daft kids to take anything up to five tablets in an evening. This is almost a death sentence, as total exhaustion is inevitable. On the other hand, there is no definite evidence that ecstasy has any nasty side-effects if taken in moderation, though, it must be said, the jury is still out on this.

CANNABIS *(dope, hash, ganja, weed, grass, shit, pot)*
Cannabis or marijuana gets most adults in terrible
arguments as many think it should be legalised while
others put it in the same boat as all the other drugs. You
can either get it as 'grass' (the leaves of the hemp plant) or
as a sticky brown resin. It is usually mixed with tobacco
and rolled in skins (cigarette papers) as 'joints' or 'spliffs'.
Both forms are fairly easily available, but you must realise
you are breaking the law to even possess it. Cannabis is
usually a teenager's first (and last) introduction to drugs
and, being illegal, could be interpreted (especially by
parents) as the stairs up to the top of the slippery slide.
Also, you must realise that it makes you prey to one of the
most powerful, greedy (and nastiest) groups of people in
the world — the dealers and the pushers.

They might very well offer you your first experience
cheap or even free, in order to get you on their fishing line.
Once they've reeled you in, they often try introducing you
to stronger stuff. Beware!

There is little proven medical evidence against cannabis
but some people, who've smoked a lot, or know someone
else who's smoked a lot, believe that it can cause mild
schizophrenia or impair your short-term memory. Now
who was it who told me that?

MAGIC MUSHROOMS

If you go out in the woods today, you could be sure of a big surprise. Around September and October there grows in many woodlands a kind of toadstool that if eaten can give you a 'trip' much like LSD. Unfortunately there are a load of other toadstools that if eaten can give a trip much like death. Magic mushrooms are legal (we couldn't have the Creator breaking the law), but if you're caught selling them you're in deep trouble.

HOW TO HANDLE YOUR PARENTS

DRUGS

1. Talk to them. Leave things around (pamphlets, magazines, etc.) that show that you might know what you're talking about. When they ask you why you've got them, tell them that you're fed up with all the lack of information, and often total bullshit, about drugs. Let them know that you want to learn what's what for yourself.

2. Ask, if you dare, about their drug experiences. If they feel that you're all in it together, they could even help you in forming your own views on the subject.

3. If they do know a lot about it, and not a whole load of half-baked nonsense, then please listen to them. Not only will it do you some good, but they will feel a lot happier too.

4. Try to establish whether you are an addictive person. Do you have binges on certain foods or get regularly pissed if there's lots of alcohol at parties? Again discuss it with Mum and Dad. Remember this kind of addictiveness can be hereditary and is not your fault.

CIGARETTES

1. If you do smoke, it won't take Inspector Morse to find out. Sooner or later they will know; so be prepared.

2. Be aware that nobody ever needs to smoke, and seeing as the first one you try will, almost definitely, taste bloody awful . . . why persist? Let's face it, if someone told you that ground-up bats' poo was really a great smoke, even if it tasted foul and would probably kill you, you'd tell them to f . . . off, go forth and multiply. Get your head round the idea that, these days, it really is well cool *NOT* to smoke.

3. If you're NOT smoking but are really worried about your mum or dad doing it, try offering them a deal. You won't start, if they stop. I know it sounds perilously close to blackmail, but so what? If it saves their lives (and more to the point, yours) how bad!

BOOZE

1. Avoid, at all costs, rolling home drunk. It will blow your 'I'm a really controlled, sensible person' cover completely. If you *are* drunk and due to be home, try to get as much air

through your lungs as possible and drink gallons of water. One of the best ways of becoming sober quickly is to walk it off.

2. Again, talk to your mum and dad. Let them know that merely talking about it means that you could be taking it seriously.

3. If ever your parents do offer you a drink, accept it (if you want one, that is). Don't pretend you don't like it just to make them feel better, or, even worse, pretend to like it just to make yourself feel grown-up.

4. One of their greatest fears will be your getting into a car with a drunk. Assure your parents (and mean it) that you will ring them if this situation occurs. (It could also be a way of staying a bit longer at a party.)

   If you do get into a car with someone who's rat-assed, you're on your own — there's nothing more anyone can do for you. One little tip. If you only realise what state your 'chauffeur' is in as he's about to pull away, pretend you feel like throwing up. Nobody wants sick all over the car (especially if it's their dad's) — not even a drunk.

5. Always tell your mum and dad if you think *they* are going over the limit for driving. If they've got any sense, they'll thank you; and more to the point, think that you've got a sensible attitude to alcohol.

Chapter 9

NEW BITS IN NEW PLACES
The trials and tribulations of growing up
physically

Parents always seem to be one step behind your physical
and mental development. Funny really, you'd think
because they see you every day, they'd be fairly clued up.
Unfortunately most people only see what they want to see
and that doesn't only apply to this specific subject.
Consequently, they might well be horrified if you
understand, let alone tell, a dirty joke, not because they
don't find it funny themselves, but because they really can't
believe you know what you're laughing at. Girls appear to
be much cooler about such things (except when talking
amongst themselves), whereas boys, who get fairly
obsessed by female parts, seem to talk and make jokes
about sex all the time. Unlike the opposite sex, boys get
turned on by 'girlie pictures' and are often very secretive
about them. Conversations like this are not unusual.

Mother:
> *"I found something rather horrible in your bedroom*
> *yesterday."*

Teenager:
> *"Sorry Mum. Did I forget to bring my plate down again?"*
> (Nice try, but you know full well what she's going on
> about.)

Mother:

> *"I'm not talking about that. It was a rather unpleasant magazine with lots of naked women in it."*

Teenager:

> *"Oh that. It's all right, it isn't mine."* (Nice one, appear casual at all times.)

Mother:

> *"I don't care whose it is, it's obscene. Why have you got it? Do you find those women attractive? They're so common and tarty; surely they aren't the sort of girls you fancy?"* (Ten out of ten for missing the point, Mum.)

Teenager:

> *"Look, I don't know. Why can't you just leave me alone?"*

Mother:

> *"You shouldn't be interested in that sort of thing at your age. I wonder what your father would say."*

Teenager (under breath):

> *"He'd probably want to borrow it."*

MOTHER'S VERSION:

Dirty little devil. How can he find those little scrubbers a turn-on? I thought he only liked nice girls. What sort of girl would display her private parts like that? Where did we go wrong? I'm sure his father never liked stuff like that, otherwise he'd never had chosen someone like me. (*Don't count on it, Madam.*) I bet it's the influence of those horrid boys he knocks around with at school. I know he wouldn't be filling his head with that muck if it wasn't for them. I wonder whether I should ring their mothers.

TEENAGER'S VERSION

Oh hell! Why didn't I hide it better? I suppose if I kept my room tidy she wouldn't have to keep going in. It's bad enough having to cope with what's happening to me,

without having her on my back. The trouble is, even I feel guilty at having mags like that, but I don't really know why.

LONG LIVE SMUT
About the only way parents have of spotting your new maturity is either from the aforementioned 'literature' or when Dad notices the hungry looks his daughter gets from boys in the street. Sex must be the only thing that most adults do regularly, but seem rather embarrassed about. It's so odd; we are totally prepared to watch people, even in the street, kissing, and even putting their tongues in each

other's mouths, but other parts of the body can only connect in private (usually with the lights out). Having said all this, perhaps it is the very fact that sex is still regarded as *rude* that makes it so much fun. Maybe if we were doing it all over the place, it wouldn't be such a big deal.

Women will never understand why most (yes most) normal males, at some time in their lives, like girlie books. They always take it so personally, thinking that in some way there's a connection in the way men think about them and the models in the mags; women as purely sexual objects etc. etc. It is true that these young models, who *seem* so blatant and available, do turn men and boys on; but it must be recognised that they are, over and above everything else, only fantasy figures. No man ever expects to go to bed with one of them, let alone take one home for tea.

SO WHY THE FUSS?

The real confusion for parents is coming to terms with your blossoming sexuality. The need for boys, especially, to masturbate is almost overwhelming, and because their knowledge of the mature female's body is often shaky, to say the least, magazines make the fantasising so much easier.

Girls, so we like to think, are much more into romance than sex, hence all those soppy boy-meets-girl comic strips in teenage magazines. Mind you, the recent phenomenal success of *The Chippendales*, that group of male bimbos with overdeveloped bodies (and underdeveloped brains), proves that there must be a market for innocent, mindless titillation for some women too. Suggest this last theory to your mother, I bet she'll tell you that those women only go there for a laugh.

74

FLASHERS

Many parents believe all this to be terribly unhealthy, but it is a fact that those who are dreadfully repressed sexually when young, stand far more chance of being the sort of weirdos who hang around public places, either flashing their parts or, much worse, molesting women and kids. Grown-ups often don't realise that teenagers (especially boys) have a sexual drive anything up to five times that of an adult.

SEX ON TELLY

Parents are quite happy to let their 'sexually naive' teenagers devour videos like *Total Recall*, where killing, maiming and gaily dismembering innocent people is all a bit of a giggle to pumped-up brick-heads like Arnold Schwartzenegger. Five minutes later, however, they'll shuffle uncomfortably, or flick over the channel, when two lusty llamas start bonking on a serious wildlife programme. You must admit it's a bit odd . . .

75

THE BIRDS AND THE BEARS

When whoever it was decided to invent the human being, he obviously thought he'd have a bit of a giggle. Unlike all of the other beasts, who all develop pretty much at the same standard rate, he thought he'd make one that was all over the shop.

If we were fish, monkeys or bears — our mums and dads (being fish, monkeys or bears themselves) would be able to tell us exactly what stage we would have developed to at any given age. Wouldn't it be nice if babies arrived with a little workshop manual which told us when we'd get the first spot (and the last), when we were going to become a bit furry, or when we would get the first uncontrolled feelings in very strange places.

For a start it would make it a lot easier for your parents to comprehend what you're going through. They'd only have to get out the old chart, flick through to your exact age and Bob's your uncle . . . instant understanding.

"Ah! it's three months after Annie's birthday, her breasts will start growing this week." Or:

"I say, I've just noticed Joe will be having his first sexual fantasies this week; better put a box of tissues in his room."

MIRROR, MIRROR ON THE WALL, WHO IS THE MATURIST OF THEM ALL?

The trouble is, as we all know, it's not quite like that. We develop at all sorts of different speeds. Of course, this wouldn't be too much of a problem if we weren't age-ist. But to teenagers, especially boys, physical maturity is the be-all and end-all.

The chap with the longest appendage always giggles at the less well-endowed and any form of body hair is greeted with wonder and reverence. Girls regard their first period as a kind of status symbol, before they realise it could become a bit of a drag.

Very often our physical development straggles along behind where our heads are. We may have a lot of very rude thoughts, for instance, but not be sure if we'd have the equipment to deal with them if the opportunity arose (if you see what I mean!!!).

HOW TO DEAL WITH YOUR PARENTS

1. Let them know, even if it's a bit embarrassing, that you are interested in the opposite sex. There are a thousand ways of letting them know that you know what they know (you know?). Laugh with them when sexual innuendos

I ONLY SAID I HAD A BIT OF A BONK IN THE BACK OF MY CAR.

crop up in everyday conversation.

2. Try not to avoid the rude bits on telly, when sitting with your mum and dad. If you go out of the room or hurriedly pick up the *TV Times*, they could think you're embarrassed and just not interested. If they try to switch channels tell them not to worry on your account. It will be a bit awkward at first but let's face it, it could well be one of the first times that you acknowledge to them the fact that you fully understand sex.

3. Introduce them to girlfriends or boyfriends as soon as possible. Boys often pretend, for some reason, that they're just not interested in girls because their parents, also for some unknown reason, take the mickey out of them if they are. If your parents are the sort that give you a hard time about boys or girls, it's because they are having a harder time accepting your growing up than you are.

4. If you have any real problems with your own physical development, and feel that you can't talk to them about it, ring up your doctor. He deals with stuff like this every day and to him it's just like taking your car to the garage.

5. Find better places to hide your dirty books.

YOU'RE NOT THE ONLY ONE
Just as you are coping with the rapid changes in your body, your parents are also having to watch, rather helplessly, changes in theirs.

MEN
When a man gets to his mid-to-late thirties funny things often start to happen. Heavy wrinkles appear where once there were lines. His chin shows signs of gaining a double; his waist mysteriously disappears; and, if he drinks beer,

he begins to get the sort of stomach which, when fully developed, makes him look like a professional darts player. Features like the nose and ears start to get mysteriously bigger and sprout hair, and his original hair starts to thin and go grey (unless he's Ronald Reagan or Bruce Forsyth). By the way, if he ever buys anything to cover up his baldness, warn him off gently. There's never been a wig (or rug) invented that you couldn't spot at fifty yards with one eye closed. To console him, relate this statistic: 50% of people will have 50% of white hair by 50.

WOMEN

Women have even more to contend with, largely due to a chauvinist society which still insists young is beautiful. Firstly there's the dreaded cellulite (a wicked fat that won't break down). The mere word seems to make women rush to the mirror and froth at the mouth. It creeps up when they're not looking and makes thighs flabby and bums wobbly. It's funny, while some women are spending fortunes having it surgically removed, other loonies are having a plastic substitute pumped into their breasts, lips and even bums to make them more rounded. But that's just the beginning. On top of this they have to contend with the same things as men — wrinkles, greying hair, thickening or thinning necks, droopy breasts (yes, even men get those), coarser skin — you name it.

Having said all this, adults generally are taking far more care of themselves these days and looking younger than their parents.

TOO BUSY

So you see, they're often too preoccupied to notice what's happening to you. If you did start to talk to them about your physical hang-ups, I bet you a night out, with the fantasy of your choice, that they wouldn't talk about theirs. Just to make things more complicated, they're probably trying to hide the changes in their bodies from each other. The whole thing is a nightmare.

The difference between your problems and theirs, however, is that you are on the way up physically and they're just beginning the long gloomy road down. It's all a question of where it's all going to end. Are you always going to have a face like the surface of the moon? Are you (if a boy) going to get so hairy that you'll only qualify for a job in a circus, or never ever need to shave? Will you (if a girl) ever have anything worth putting in a bra, or always have legs like lolly sticks?

Chapter 10

INTO THE LIONS' DEN
Meeting the parents

Isn't life strange. For years nothing you ever do seems right to your mum and dad, but there's an about turn when you bring a boyfriend (or girlfriend) home for the very first time. It's as if you've suddenly become a little angel, and the 'interloper', the devil incarnate. Daughters always get a much harder time than sons over this one and conversations often go like this:

Father:

> *"So that was the Dominic we've been hearing all about. I must admit we were a bit surprised."*

Teenager:

> *"Why? Didn't you think he was great?"* (Now just who are you kidding? You were actually there.)

Father:

> *"That's hardly the word I'd use. He didn't say a single word. All we had to go on were his looks, and, let's face it, he'll never win the 'Best Dressed Boy of Britain' competition."* (Who wants to look like that anyway?)

Teenager:

> *"Dad, you're such a hypocrite. You always told me never to judge a book by its cover. Dominic's great when you get to know him."*

Father:

> *"You're kidding. He seemed like a rather dog-eared cover with no book in it."*

Teenager:

> *"You're so horrible to me. I can't think what sort of boy you would approve of. He'd have to be a sort of teenage Cliff Richard."* (And who wouldn't want him as a son-in-law?)

Father:

> *"Well I suppose if you like him, there's not much more to say about it, but I really thought you could do a bit better than that."* (Trust him to say just one more thing about it.)

Teenager (under the breath):

> *"You forget. I've got something huge going against me. Dreadful, hypocritical parents!"*

PARENT'S VIEW
Oh dear, oh dear. I just can't bear the idea of that spotty little oik getting his hands on my little girl. How could she find that thing attractive. I've met more stimulating tortoises. It wouldn't be so bad if he had something to say for himself, but all he did was look gormless and stare at the floor. I don't expect her to go out with a goody-goody, or a world class orator *(actually he'd be much happier if she didn't go out with anyone)* but I do expect the kid she chooses to have a bit of personality.

TEENAGER'S VIEW
Well that was a huge success. Why couldn't they give poor Dom a break? It wouldn't take a genius to realise that he's just a bit shy with grown-ups. It's so unfair, he's such a gas when he's out with our mates. Honestly, they seem to look

for ways of making me mad. That's the last time I ever bring anyone home to meet them. I don't give a damn about what they think any more.

PARENT POWER

Oh yes, you do, that's the trouble. Isn't it weird. You disagree with just about everything your parents say or stand for, but still seem to seek their approval. This, you'll be depressed to learn, usually goes on until adult life. Perhaps the definition of a fully paid-up, really proper, free-standing grown-up, is someone who, at last, isn't remotely influenced by their parents' opinion. That's true independence. Some poor devils never achieve this and are dominated by their parents all their lives, even if they've got married and had kids of their own.

If you are about to present the love of your life (God help you) to your parents, or even worse, about to enter the lions' den yourself, there are a few things you can do to make it bearable. You never know, they might even actually like you.

HOW TO HANDLE PARENTS

1. Try, try, try to talk. Anything's better than silence. There's nothing worse than someone who simply mumbles one-word answers.

2. Don't, for heaven's sake, whisper among yourselves when in a room with the parents. That really is guaranteed to get up their noses.

3. Don't be scared of them. In a funny way they could be more scared of you. For all they know, you might be going to lead their little precious astray (with a bit of luck).

4. If you're a boy, you can bet your bottom dollar that your girlfriend's dad will be thinking that all you want to do is

84

get your grubby hands on his daughter. This may well be true, but for goodness' sake don't begin to do it in front of them. Try and keep at least six inches apart on the first encounter. You never know, they might think it's just platonic.

5.   Try and tone down your appearance for the first couple of visits. If you like looking like one of the *Furry Freak Brothers* remember that they almost certainly won't. Life will be a lot easier if you make a reasonable first impression.

WHICH ONE'S OURS?

Chapter 11

SEX FOR THE FIRST TIME
How, why, when and who with

You'd better get used to the idea. Parents and their offspring will always have problems when sex rears its ugly (depending which way you look at it) head.
No matter what age you or they are, talking about sex is like wading through a field of treacle. It is hard enough for some parents to describe to children where little babies come from, and now you're a teenager it's even harder to discuss 'doing it'. My parents were so embarrassed about the whole subject that, as it was never even mentioned, I wouldn't have been at all surprised if I was the Second Coming, born to a virgin mother. To all intents and purposes, they led me to believe (through total lack of information) that they had actually never done *it*. Even at the ripe old age of sixteen, I was still trying to piece the final details together.

SEX — YUKK!
The hang-up most parents have is quite simple. They find it almost impossible to communicate that the concept of sticking what their little ones regard as one rude bit into another rude bit, and then jiggling it around, can possibly be any fun for either party. They know that most youngsters will think that it's some terrible chore that at some time they'll have to go through in order to make babies. As the child becomes older, the more technical it all

becomes, and the worse it seems to get. All those books with drawings of what looks like soft, pink engine parts or the cold, rather scientific approach you get taught at school, give the young the idea that one needs a set of instructions to know what to do. Still, this is better than all the dodgy stuff your schoolmates might tell you. All this to describe what the opposite sexes have been doing since time began. My goodness, it's enough to put us all off! By now, at your advanced age, you are probably wondering what all the fuss is about. After all, with the notable exception (reputedly!) of the aforementioned Joseph and Mary, the opposite sexes have been at *it* since they were grovelling around in the primeval slime resembling something like tadpoles.

SORRY EMMA. I FORGOT THE INSTRUCTIONS

It all stems from the fact that parents have had you from new, so to speak. To them you are still partly the innocent little baby that they loved and cherished. It seems only a few years ago that they leaned over your cot making dumb sounds like goo-goo and ga-ga, and even less that they were telling you daft stories about stupid bunny rabbits and little baa-lambs. I suppose the idea of suddenly switching from all that so-called baby-friendly dialogue to the ins and outs of sex (whoops!) is almost too much for the average parent to bear.

CUT THE CRAP DAD WHERE DID I COME FROM?

THE NEXT STEP

After having explained the facts of life, the next hurdle for parents to handle is the stage you are at now. It's one thing telling your kids *how* to do *it*, and what happens if you do, but it's another facing the prospect that imminently they actually might!

Teenager (girl):

"Mum, I was wondering about going on the pill. Who should I see about it?"

Mother:

"Are you joking? You're far too young. Why should you possibly need to do something like that? You haven't been going too far with that Ben, I hope."

Teenager:

"Of course not, it's just in case." (Do you feel your nose getting a little longer?)

Mother:

"In case of what? I think I'd better ring his mother."

(Better than wringing his neck, I suppose.)

Teenager:

> *"Oh no please don't, I'd look a right idiot. Stop treating*
> *me like a kid. Sooner or later we're going to want to do it.*
> *It's better that I take precautions now, before it's too late."*

(If it's not already.)

Mother:

> *"No, I'm sorry, you're just too young. I'm sure your father*
> *would agree with me."*

MOTHER'S VIEW

Damn, that caught me right on the hop. I never expected
that she was anywhere near that stage. What should we do
for the best? The trouble is, if we stop her she'll just do it
anyway and then we'd have an abortion on our hands. This
is almost blackmail. I was eighteen before I even thought of
proper sex. What will her father think? God, he'll go
through the roof when I tell him. He still sees her as his
baby. I doubt whether he even realises she's fully mature
sexually let alone poised on the brink. Let's hope this thing
with Ben is just another five-minute wonder like all the
others. With a bit of luck there'll be someone else in a
couple of weeks.

TEENAGER'S VIEW

Talk about keeping your head in the sand. I expect she
thinks we play doctors and bloody nurses when I go round
to Ben's house. She and dad would burst a blood vessel if
they knew that we'd already done it, and that it was a very
near thing. Why can't they accept that times have changed,
and people don't wait until they've got a wedding ring,
and somewhere to live, before they get it together?
Anyway, why can't they realise that I really love Ben and
there'll never be anyone else?

89

THE BIG DILEMMA

Most parents are completely at sea when it comes to situations like this. If they seem to be happy about you taking precautions, they worry in case they seem to be encouraging you to get at it like rabbits. On the other hand, if they go too heavy the other way they worry that you'll go and do it unprotected and get into all kinds of grief. What they forget is that the intensity of passion you feel when young is probably stronger than anything you might feel later. OK it might not always last long, but teenagers seldom sleep with more than one person (one's complicated enough).

Much as it could be your intention to get *it* over with as soon as possible, you can bet your bottom dollar that it will be their intention to prevent you for as long as possible. Bear in mind, however, there is no such word as *ready* where sex is concerned. All I suggest is that when you actually get round to *it*, you do it with:

a. Someone you really like (which rules out quick bonks with someone you just met).

b. Someone you trust (who isn't going to tell the whole neighbourhood).

c. Someone you are pretty sure you will want to see
    again after the event (and who will want to see you).

T-T-T-TIMING
Remember this. There's plenty of time for the real thing,
and there are lots of really brilliant things you can do (use
your imagination) without going the whole way. Don't let
your friends make you feel a sissy if you haven't yet
(chances are they're lying anyway); and if you really must,
USE A CONDOM! Anyone who doesn't, needs their brains
(and their blood) tested.

Firstly, if you're worried that it's never ever going to
happen to you, take heart. 70% of teenage girls and 80% of
teenage boys have done it at least once before leaving their
teens. What ever happened to the 10%?

BUT HOW DO I TELL MY PARENTS?
If you think the reaction is going to bring the roof down,
you don't *have* to tell them. Some parents would genuinely

91

prefer not to know. Others, however, most certainly would and only you can know which sort you've got.

Let's first define the major fears that parents have relating to you and sex:

1.   That you've actually done *it* already.

2.   That you've done *it*, or look like you're about to do *it* with someone they disapprove of. (Be warned, your dad would probably disapprove of Prince bloody Charming if he thought he was going to lay a hand on his daughter.)

3.   That they haven't given you enough real information to protect yourself if it does happen. It's no good shutting the stable door after the horse has bolted.

4.   That you might get hurt. You might not be emotionally ready, and have been forced into it and may be dumped when you've done it.

HOW TO HANDLE YOUR PARENTS
1.   If things are beginning to get heavy with your boyfriend, bite on the bullet and discuss it with whichever parent you believe would be most sympathetic. It's like jumping into a swimming pool. The prospect seems horrible at first, but once you're in it's not so bad.

Notice I only used a girl in this example. Parents don't seem to worry nearly so much about boys, probably because we still live in a sexist society in which the male, being the 'giver', doesn't suffer the same consequences as the 'receiver'.

2.   If either one of them asks, out of the blue, if you've done *it*, for God's sake say yes (if you have). There'll never be a better opportunity to come clean. If you keep denying it, especially if you use that injured 'how-could-you-think-I'd-

do-such-a-thing' voice, it will make things far worse later. Many kids dig themselves into such a pit of self-righteousness that their parents start thinking that there might actually be something wrong with them.

3. This requires all your acting skills. Choose the more nervous of your parents and tell them that you have to talk with them immediately. Effect a look of real deranged panic in your eyes (practise in front of a mirror). This, with a bit of luck, will get them in such a state that anything short of crashing Dad's car, murdering a policeman, or becoming (or getting someone) pregnant will seem like a blessed relief.

"Oh is that all, darling, I thought it was something really serious. Was it nice?"

Of course this is the optimistic reaction. If you don't do it dramatically enough, or they're the sort of parents who'd throw a fit over treading on the flower beds, then you might find yourself confined to barracks for a few weeks.

Seriously though, whatever reaction they have (or you think they will have), be brave; like day follows night, if they love you, they'll come round in the end.

ON THE OTHER HAND
If you have parents who pretend that sex is only for making babies, or would rush to the chastity belt shop if you even looked at the opposite sex, it might be wiser to keep the fact that you're already bonking away from their delicate ears. Be careful, though, there are certain give-away signs that you're 'in love' or doing *it* that observant parents should spot quite easily:

1. Daughter comes home with a stupid grin on face walking at least six inches above the ground.

2. Son swaggers in and says "How's it going, mate?" to his father.

3. Daughter spends hours gazing at bedroom ceiling, having torn all her pin-ups off the wall.

4. Suddenly son has a brand new condom packet under the mattress instead of the old, battered, past-its-use-by-date one.

5. Daughter uses the phone about four times more than usual to discuss it endlessly with her best friend.

6. Both sexes suddenly become incredibly matter-of-fact when talking about their respective partners.

7. Either sex comes in looking sheepish or just plain disappointed, as if they'd found a pound and then lost twenty. (So that was what all the fuss was about!)

Chapter 12

AN ALIEN IN THE HOUSE
A new mummy or daddy

There can be very few situations in life as gut-wrenchingly difficult as having a strange man (or woman) coming into *your* house, sleeping with *your* mother (or father), and then, after a little while, telling *you* how to run *your* life. If anything like that happened in the animal kingdom, there'd be blood spilt before dawn. Not only is it difficult for you, but also for the parent who's introducing the new person, and, it must be said, for the new person him- or herself. As

mothers usually get custody of the children (which could be called the booby prize) we'll use a new man in the house as our example:

Mother:

"*Mark darling, you could at the very least try a little harder to make Neville welcome. It's not easy for him you know . . .*"

Teenager:

"*C'mon Mum. It's his choice. I didn't have a say in it.*"

Mother:

"*I asked you if you'd mind and, when you just shrugged, I thought that meant yes.*" (This must be the most imaginative guessing at body language known to man or woman.)

Teenager:

"*Yeah! That was before I realised he was such a prat. I just don't understand how you could fancy a guy like that, he's such a wimp.*"

Mother:

"*He is not a wimp. You're so cruel. Just because he's quiet and sensitive and doesn't throw his weight around, unlike someone who used to live here.*" (Could that possibly be a reference to your late, great, dear-departed father?)

Teenager:

"*Just let him try. This is our house. It's his job to fit in with us. He's not my new dad and never will be.*"

Mother:

"*You're so hard. Neville thinks the world of you. Why can't you at least give him a chance?*"

Teenager:

"*Look, I'll try. But don't try to make me stick around while he's playing his Richard Clayderman collection, or ask me to carry his stupid clubs round the golf course.*"

AN ALIEN IN THE HOUSE

MOTHER'S VERSION

Cunning little devil. He knows he's got me by the short and curlies, and that he holds my happiness with Nev in the palm of his grubby little hand. I bet he's going to milk this one for all it's worth. He treats poor Nev like someone from another planet, sometimes totally ignoring him — rude little bugger! It's just not fair. His dad would have knocked him into the middle of next week if he'd behaved like that then; whereas Neville, bless him, bends over backwards to be understanding. He can only take so much, however, and I've got a terrible feeling that pretty soon he'll snap. Maybe the sooner the better. Sometimes I think my son resents him coming along and making me happy. It's so unfair.

TEENAGER'S VERSION

Jeeesus, what a creep! How could she do it? How could she go out with someone called Neville in the first place? How could she let him near her body? Urghh! And as for all those terrible jokes: if I found them in Christmas crackers I'd ask for my money back; and all that trying to be my mate and understanding-what-it's-like-to-be-a-teenager crap. Blimey, it's difficult to believe he was ever one. He even made out he liked our band, *Rockweillers on Acid*. We must be losing our touch. It would be better if he was just his awful self, at least we'd know where the battle lines really were.

I thought life in this house was bad enough during the cold war, when Dad was around, but he was nothing compared with this jerk — if I was wrecked on a desert island with him, I'd end up eating him. It's so unfair.

LOVE OR MARRIAGE

These days getting married is a bit like buying a second-hand car. It looks great when you first get in it (pardon the metaphor), but there are seldom any guarantees that it will get you to where you want to go.

If you're into betting, don't put your money on the longevity of a marriage these days. The odds are three to one against it going into the sunset. Having said that, the odds on remarrying are much better — 78% for women and 83% for men, and that usually happens pretty soon after the divorce. Amazing really, to the cynic it's a bit like buying a dog that eventually bites your hand off; and then, as soon as it's been got rid of, going out and buying another one.

RED CARPET?

All this means is that, if your parents are breaking up, or are just about to, you can expect the patter of rather large feet coming through the front door pretty damn soon. If you've already experienced it, you will probably agree it's a bit like a herring deciding to live in a penguin pool. There's a fair chance that whichever way it turns, it will be disastrous.

I mean, you might have thought your parents were crass, past their sell-by date, boring and bossy, but at least they *were* your parents, which gave them a sort of right to be. I suppose it's just a case of better the Neville you know than the Neville you don't.

NO SOLUTION

There really isn't any good answer to this one. However wonderful the 'interloper' is, he (or she) can seldom replace the one that's gone. Having said that, if the dear departed was a real pain, practically anything would be better than that. If you've been going through a mini Falklands war for months and maybe years, having someone in the house who really likes your remaining parent and treats them well could be pretty good (albeit a bit stomach-turning). Well that's the theory anyway.

HOW TO HANDLE THE SITUATION

1. Try to work out whether the new person is *really* a creep or is just appearing to be so because of the difficulty of the situation. If they have sons and daughters, try and talk to them about things. They will tell you much more. Remember, they will probably be thinking the same about your mum or dad.

2. For the first month or so everyone will be walking on eggshells, trying not to upset one another. As time goes by the atmosphere will start to settle down. Don't rock the boat too soon.

3. Try to encourage the parent that you're living with to play the field a bit. One of the great dangers of their vulnerable situation is that they fall hook, line and sinker for the first person that shows them any affection. If they do settle down with that first person, they could, within another year or so, be in exactly the same mess that they were in before.

4. Beware if the new person in the house appears to be too lenient, letting you get away with everything. It might seem brill at first, but a certain amount of strictness can sometimes be a good thing. It shows a certain strength and leadership which (a) shows that they care and
(b) could come in useful if you ever get into some deep water later on.

Chapter 13

POOR OLD PARENTS
What life's like for them in the naughty nineties

Not seeing eye to eye with your parents is not only a British syndrome, it goes on all over the world. Eskimo kids probably get as hard a time if they slide home late to the igloo as Japanese kids do if they don't bow to their

DO YOU KNOW THE TIME?
IT'S QUARTER PAST WINTER

fathers etc. Parents usually believe that they should command respect. Not necessarily from what they do, but purely because you owe it to them that you're here. Is this argument familiar?

Father:
"Why don't you ever believe what I tell you is for the best? It's as if my age and experience counts for nothing."

Teenager:

> *"Oh come on Dad, look at the state your generation have left the planet in. Global warming, acid rain, half the world with too much food and the other half with none. A country in full recession because everyone grabbed too much under a government that only looked after you if you played the yuppie game. Yes, Dad — brilliant."*

Father:

> *"Don't be so damn cheeky. We used to respect our parents. If I had spoken to my father like that he'd have got his belt out."*

Teenager:

> *"Yes, that's the way I would expect most grown-ups would really prefer to solve arguments."* (Careful, this is getting close to the mark.)

Father:

> *"You just don't realise what it's like bringing up a family these days. A bit of co-operation wouldn't go amiss sometimes. When I think what your mother and I went without to give you the best."*

Teenager (under breath):

> *"Oh no! Not that old 'you're-so-lucky' chestnut again. Please, oh Lord, if I ever find myself saying such crap, strike me dead."*

PARENT'S VIEW

Ungrateful little monkey. He treats this place like a hotel, me like a meal ticket and his mother like a housemaid. I can't get over how he's changed. I hardly recognise that lovely little chap I used to play football with in the park. All he seems to be interested in now is seeing how little he can do around the house, how much he can squeeze out of me, and how much he can annoy us with his filthy habits. If I had known then what I know now I'd have invented the vasectomy myself.

TEENAGER'S VIEW

I don't know if I can stand much more of this. He still treats me as a six-year-old; no wonder I can never tell him anything. He really believes that the older you get the cleverer you become. I wonder if Einstein had this problem with his dad.

He seems to know nothing about what's going on these days, apart from his bloody job and who's doing what to who at the golf club. It's all right for him, he's through the difficult bit. Why can't he just lie back, enjoy it . . . *and leave me alone.*

IS THERE LIFE AFTER FORTY?
Being a teenager is pretty tricky at the best of times, but being a fully paid-up, no-excuses-any-more adult in the nasty nineties is often not much easier. Just so that you can understand why they seem never to have been young, let me outline a few of the things your parents (unless they know something I don't) are up against.

After hours of complex calculations I've just concluded that if you are between thirteen and say seventeen, and your parents had you when they were between, say, at the youngest twenty (unless they're stark, staring bonkers) and forty, then they must be between say thirty-three and fifty-three now (all Nobel prizes gratefully received). As you're rushing, like a rat up a drain, to achieve an age where you'll be taken seriously, your poor old mum and dad are hanging on by their fingertips to the last vestiges of their youth. It's funny really, there must be this mythical age to which all teenagers aspire. A kind of brilliant plateau where not only do you look your best, but have lots of your own money and limitless self-confidence.

It's tempting to compare it with conquering a vast mountain. You climb and climb for weeks until, eventually, you get to the very top. What do you do then? You sit around for a few minutes, get well bored and then start coming all the way back down again.

The trouble with growing up is that you never know where the bloody top is, or when you've reached it — until suddenly you find yourself sliding down the other side, looking back nostalgically to where you've come from. And that's where your mum and dad almost certainly are now, poor old things.

A PERFECT WORLD

The media don't help. So much of what you see on telly promotes a kind of perfect world. Sometimes one forgets they're just actors, and gets lured into thinking that most other families are happy and smiling, treating each other with understanding and respect from dawn to dusk.
It might interest you to note that there are hardly ever any teenagers in advertisements. Ad agencies aren't stupid. Most households containing teenagers have to cope with periodic tensions that reduce all concerned to quivering wrecks.

As far as soaps and sitcoms are concerned, about the only one that seems to ring true is *Roseanne* from the States. The writers and actors have managed to capture that often embarrassing, often explosive, often sullen, often hilarious atmosphere of a house at war.

MONEY MATTERS?

Money must be one of the all-time boring subjects, but one that creeps into every aspect of our lives. Just think how quickly you get through your pocket, or birthday, money. Well, just multiply this by goodness-knows-what and you might get some angle on how much it costs to run a family like yours (unless you happen to live in a cardboard box).

But why should you be grateful for all they've done (and do) for you? After all, no one begged them to produce you all those years ago. But, before you swear at your personal adults the next time they turn down your request for an £80 pair of trainers (trainers for what? I ask), or tell you to cut down on your telephone calls to the boy or girl only next door, make sure that they are not some of the millions of parents that have suffered so dreadfully from this damn recession. If they're not having a hard time you're lucky. For most families, from whatever class or income bracket, the downturn in the economy has crept up, like a snake in the grass, and bitten them where it hurts most — the wallet.

Whether your father (or mother) has a high-powered job dragging home loads of dosh, or is on the dole, going bankrupt, or even banged up in prison, he is bound to notice his spending power severely torpedoed. Next time you have to go on supermarket duty with Mum or Dad take a quick squint at the final bill at the check-out. £60? — £70? — £80? — £100? Think about it. This isn't a one-off. This happens every week, and is only a fraction of the outgoings. Everything you do in the house costs, right down to the last sheet of loo paper or the final flake of corn. A family is like an ever-widening mouth. The more you shove down it, the more it wants.

Every month, like night follows day, the blasted bill grows, usually (like a bucket with a hole in) faster than the amount of money coming in.

SEX AND PARENTS (GULP)
Minefield time! I expect the idea of your mum and dad actually doing *it* is a bit weird. I mean, why should they? How *can* they still fancy each other after all those years?

Sustaining a healthy and, dare I say, fun sex life for a long time is not easy. Half the fun of sex is not knowing what your partner's going to do next. This unpredictability, I'm sad to say, tends to wear a bit thin after a few years. Let's face it, it's a bit like playing a new computer game. At first it's exciting and brill, but as soon as one beats it or knows its limits, the fascination goes. Obviously the need to rip each other's clothes off at every given opportunity has passed, and all the boring routine of everyday living seems to squash that early heady romance. The trouble is that love doesn't really enter into this equation. This is when husbands and wives sometimes (well, more often than sometimes) start noticing the opposite sex with a rekindled interest (often known as the seven-year itch).

You can still worship the ground your husband or wife walks on but lust after the woman or man over the road. But the law, society and your partner (on pain of a slow, lingering death) demand that you only have one at a time (swizz!). You may look but not touch. Actually, nine times out of ten you're not even allowed to look.

AM I STILL FANCIABLE?
On top of all this most men and women, after about thirty, seem to need a great deal of reassurance that they are still attractive. Unfortunately the last person to give you that assurance (even if they wanted to) is the old husband or wife.

109

POOR OLD PARENTS

If you think about it, one spends such a great deal of one's early life chasing or being chased by the opposite sex that it comes as quite a blow to the system when it all stops.

OK. MAYBE I'M NOT THE FAIREST ANY MORE.

AFFAIR TIME

Affairs are both parties' fault, and certainly not yours. Nor are bad marriages either. No one is ever involved with someone else unless they're good and ready. Married people whose partners are found to be having an affair often want to murder the other party. This is stupid and pointless — just a futile and unrealistic gesture. After all, as the old saying goes, 'it takes two to tango'. If the relationship was still firing on all cylinders, there would be no question of unfaithfulness in the first place.

HEALTH

By now your grandparents are beginning to show slight signs of wearing out. This might not be that much of a hassle for you, but for your parents (their children) it's a savage reminder of their mortality.

It's around now that all the little complaints that are to bug them for the rest of their lives (like a five-year-old car) begin to subtly present themselves. Energy levels start to wane slightly, often compensated for by vicious attacks of exercise. You shouldn't laugh. There's nothing sadder than those middle-aged joggers half creeping, half stumbling along the street in brand new tracksuits that will shortly be relegated to gardening. They'd do far better to look at the real killer — stress, which lurks behind every unpaid bill and missed promotion.

Anyone who tells you that ageing is a wonderful enriching experience is talking through their hat.

So you see, life's not all champagne and roses for the old ones. Many of their expectations, either career-wise or personally, will by now have been dashed, and on top of all that, they can't even begin to work out where you're at head-wise or anything else-wise.

HOW TO HANDLE YOUR PARENTS

1. Look for signs of stress. If they are having a hard time financially, try to adjust your demands accordingly. Believe it or not, most parents *do* hate depriving their kids of those little luxuries that, at the time, you don't think you can live without (like Nintendo computer games and hundred-quid trainers).

2. If you can help boost you own pocket money, with a paper round or Saturday job, it will show them that you don't think that money grows on trees.

3. Try to let them in on your problems. They might not be able to help directly, but a problem shared is a problem halved.

SORRY OFFICER, WE'VE NEVER SEEN HER BEFORE!

4. Get it into your head that your parents aren't infallible. After all, they're not another species; just two human beings like you, thirty or so years on, trying in their way to make head or tail of it all.

112

Chapter 14

A TO Z OF THINGS YOUR PARENTS ARE ALWAYS GOING ON ABOUT

ABBA:
Awful Swedish band that won the equally awful
Eurovision Song Contest in 1974, and went on to make
several awful hit records. Famed for wearing clothes that,
however much they tried, always looked like they came
from a ten-year-old dressing-up box.

BAY CITY ROLLERS:
A Scottish teenybopper band that came and went before
you could put on your tartan braces, trousers and scarf
(worn around the waist). In spite of their incomprehensible
popularity (and incomprehensible lyrics), challenge your
mum and dad to remember just one of their hits.

BEATLEMANIA:
A phenomenon never before seen on such a scale
throughout the world. Girls from all walks of life literally
wet their knickers and foamed at the mouth over the four
lads from Liverpool. When they appeared on the *Ed
Sullivan* show in the States to an audience of 75,000,000, it
was reported that not one crime was committed by a
teenager. *Beatlemania* died away when they started
squabbling among themselves.

BEATNIKS:
Art-school-based teenagers from around the early sixties to
the early seventies, who followed traditional jazz and folk
music (see *Bob Dylan*). They were the first to grow their hair
long and wear black all the time. Boys would often don
black corduroy suits, white rounded stiff collars and dark
shirts. They also re-invented the elastic sided boots that
became known as *Chelsea Boots* (favoured by the great *Vic
Reeves*).

When bored they would go on the road; which meant
travelling around the country with no more than a sleeping
bag and a guitar, for no apparent reason. They turned
eventually into hippies and now those travellers in old
coaches that the police delight in always moving on.

BEN SHERMAN:
An American soft cotton shirt favoured by the *Mods* and
Skinheads. It had a soft, button-down collar and was usually
lightly striped.

BEST — GEORGIE:
One of the few footballers ever to reach pop star status.
Golden boy of *Manchester United* in the late sixties and
seventies, poor Georgie fell prey to wine, women and song
with the emphasis on the wine and women. Despite several
attempts at a comeback (as a footballer), he just became an
embarrassing icon of the era.

BIBA:
A wacky but stylish clothes shop opened in *Church Street,
Kensington* by *Barbara Hulaniki* in 1964. Cheap, rather badly
made, but desperately *in* garments took over mass fashion

for nearly a decade. From shop workers (see *Twiggy*) to debutantes (see *debutantes*), every girl would aspire to their often daring new look. Tightly-fitting dresses in black and purple, ostrich-feather boas, platform shoes and huge twenties-style hats were so popular that young girls would often queue outside the relatively small store. Biba died when it 'went big' and became a department store. Apparently the combination of the poorly-paid staff nicking all the clothes, and the new store becoming a (non-buying) tourist attraction proved too much.

BLOW-UP:
If you want to see what your parents looked like in the days of 'Swinging London' watch the film *Blow-Up* starring *David Hemmings*. It was one of the first films to show nudity, albeit tame by today's standards, and a new, free attitude to sex that shocked grown-ups.

BLUE BEAT:
Forerunner of ska and reggae. West Indian dance music popular in or around 1970. One of the only national hits was *My Boy Lollipop* by *Milly*. During this period there was very little racial tension and *Blue-Beat* parties in South London would often have an equal mix of black and white.

BOSTON:
Haircut adopted by many middle-of-the-road young men in the early- to mid-sixties. Hair was cut and shaved in a straight line at the back.

BROTHEL CREEPERS:
Suede shoes worn by teddyboys and still on sale today.
They have crêpe soles, often extremely thick, a bit like the
teds who used to wear them.

BUBBLE CARS:
Strange, tiny two-seater cars from Germany which were to
answer the growing traffic problem in the late fifties and
early sixties. If you didn't mind looking a total prat, they
were a good, cheap way to travel.

BUM-FREEZERS:
Italian suits with short jackets, no turn-ups and tiny lapels
favoured by the teenage mods in the sixties.

CAVERN CLUB:
Horrible, sweaty, underground club in Liverpool where the
Beatles and the *Mersey Sound* first started.

CLARK — OSSIE:
Just about the most famous 70s British high fashion

designer, who disappeared into oblivion by the end of the decade.

CLAY — CASSIUS:
Ridiculously good-looking black boxer who caught religion and turned into *Mohammed Ali*. His slogan was 'Float like a butterfly, sting like a bee'. Poor Mohammed fought one fight too many and was badly stung. He slurred his speech from then on.

COFFEE BARS:
Before teenagers got stuck into pubs, most young people in the fifties and sixties hung out in coffee bars. It all started when the first frothy-coffee machines came over from Italy.

COLLEGE BOY:
A short hair-cut worn by the mods.

COURRÈGES:
French designer who with *Hulaniki* and *Mary Quant* shaped the fashion of the late sixties. Black and white shiny mini-

skirts and dresses, high plastic boots, dresses with windows all flooded into the department stores and onto the British streets.

CREAM:
Cult rock band of the late sixties and early seventies. *Eric Clapton, Jack Bruce* and *Ginger Baker* rode high amongst the *in* bands until the demon drugs allegedly got the better of them.

CURTIS — TONY:
Hairstyle adopted by the teddyboys through the fifties and early sixties. It consisted of a huge curl or quiff at the front and a DA (duck's ass) at the back.

DEBUTANTES:
Daughters of the aristocracy who were brought out (into society) before leaving their teens. They were presented before the Queen. It was also a kind of meat market for them to meet, and get hitched up with, eligible men. The practice, although officially abandoned, still exists to a lesser extent.

DENTON CHISELPOINTS:
A strange shoe of the sixties, born out of the *Winklepicker*. It had a long pointy toe with the end lopped off straight like a chisel. It was often bought by teenagers (like me) to get round parents who wouldn't let them have pointed shoes.

DOORS:
Semi-underground band that became a cult when *Jim Morrison* died of a drug overdose. Their music sounds contemporary even today.

DYLAN — BOB:
Cult hero of the *Beatniks* and *folkies* through the sixties. He committed the greatest sin when he 'went electric' in the early seventies. Still, it didn't seem to do his career that much harm.

EP:
A cross between a single and an album, having four tracks, two on each side.

EVEL KNEIVEL:
Daft American stuntman who started the insane craze for jumping over big things on motorbikes. By the time he retired he'd broken (and had fixed) just about every bone in his body. I think they should have started by examining his head.

FAITHFULL — MARIANNE:
A nice convent girl who discovered pop music, drugs and Mick Jagger. Would have been forgotten had it not been for an incident with a well-known chocolate bar at one of the *Rolling Stones'* infamous parties (allegedly). It certainly helped her work, rest and play.

FLARES:
Weird trousers adopted by the hippies. They started low on the hip, were revealingly skintight to the knee, and flared out to up to thirty-inch bottoms. There is a movement to bring them back as I write. If you want to look hyper-trendy (and hyper-daft), be my guest.

FRENCH-JIVE:
A strange dance to traditional jazz, practised by *Beatniks*. A version was called the *Cy Laurie* after an early sixties jazz

band leader. It involved the girl running up and down like a mad thing while the guy just stood there and held her hand!

GREAT TRAIN ROBBERS:
A group of very naughty chaps who held up a mail train in 1963 and nicked £2,500,000. It was the best (sorry! worst) rail robbery ever. Strangely enough everyone, if they'd been honest, had to admire them for their audacity. Gradually they were all caught, including *Ronnie Biggs*, one of the ring leaders, who eventually escaped to South America and thumbed his nose to the British police who weren't allowed to go and get him.

GREEN — HUGHIE:
Loud, annoying Canadian who never seemed to be off the telly in the sixties and seventies. His most famous programme was *Opportunity Knocks*, a talent contest for strangely talentless people. If you could stand on one leg, wearing a tutu while plucking a chicken and playing *Land of Hope and Glory* on the bagpipes, this was the vehicle for you.

HAIGHT-ASHBURY:
A part of San Francisco which became Mecca for all the hippies. Practically everyone had flowers in their hair, smoked lots of wacky baccy, wore trillions of beads and practised peace and love in huge quantities (particularly the latter).

HAND-JIVE:
This will really embarrass your mum and dad. Ask them to show you the hand-jive. This was a strange series of hand and arm actions practised in the late sixties to accompany pop music. The advantage (if you can call it such) was that you could do it sitting down.

HENDRIX — JIMI:
A wild American, who symbolised the acid-soaked seventies. Strangely enough, he only really made it in Britain. What he didn't do with his guitar was nobody's business; burning it, bashing it, playing behind his back, biting it — you name it, he did it. He died, at only 24, from choking on his own vomit after an acid trip. Charming, eh?

HOT PANTS:
Arguably the silliest (albeit sexiest) fashion item of the early seventies. Tight shorts, that left nothing to the imagination, replaced mini-skirts and maxi-skirts for one or two very short summers. It didn't look bad on girls with long slim legs, but what percentage of the female population is so blessed?

HULA-HOOPS:
When your mum and dad were kids, a craze came over from the States that swept through the country like Asian flu. Huge plastic hoops that one swivelled round one's

waist, for some reason were bought by young and old alike. They had championships and endurance contests and at one point you couldn't drive down any street without seeing some lunatic hula-hooping away to his heart's content. Bizarre!

IVY LEAGUE:
Little-known but hyper-trendy fashion amongst teenage boys in the late sixties and early seventies. While hippies were busy turning on and tuning out, and mods were still fighting rockers, these lads would be dressing in all-American clothes, based on an ultra-cool college boy look. Very pale colours, seersucker striped jackets, brown brogues or loafers, button down shirts and slim ties. The Beach Boys took over as the fashion gurus for this group. The surfing sound became their music and surfing their sport.

KER-KNOCKERS:
Ask your parents if they remember these from 1971. Would you believe it, these were two plastic balls on a length of string which were swung against each other (ouch) making a loud cracking noise, and became as big a craze as the *Yoyo* and the *Hula-hoop*.

KIPPER TIES:
Shaped like the popular if somewhat smelly fish, these appalling ties were the height of fashion in the early seventies. You might even find one in your dad's wardrobe. They were often up to four inches across at the bottom with floral patterns that looked like a badly adjusted colour telly. They were worn with shirts with dreadful long collars and desperately unflattering suits in colours like lavender and salmon pink. These suits were not only waisted but had huge flappy lapels and flared trousers. The whole look must rank high in the annals of bad fashion.

LOCOMOTION:
A dance craze that lasted about ten minutes. It came from a record by *Little Eva* called, believe it or not, *The Locomotion*. It involved going round the dance floor imitating a train. That should make the old parents blush.

LORD LUCAN:
In 1974 a very naughty Lord murdered his family's nanny and wounded his wife. It started the most famous manhunt (or Lord-hunt) ever, and to this day, despite having been 'seen' in just about every country in the world, he's never been caught.

THIS SHOULD FOOL 'EM. —

EMIGRATION

THE MADISON:
Another weird dance that came and went in the late sixties.
It involved loads of teenagers lining up on the dance floor
and strolling a couple of steps forward, crossing their legs,
and then taking a couple of steps back. This went on for
hours and, strangely enough, I never met anyone who
enjoyed it very much.

MAGIC ROUNDABOUT:
A strange, low-key, stop-frame puppet series that caught
the imagination of kids and adults alike when it hit the telly
in 1970. *Zebedee*, a kind of Jack-in-the-box (without the box)
and *Dougal*, a mop on wheels (reckoned to be a dog)
became almost national heroes.

MAHARISHI YOGI:
King of the hippie gurus. The *Beatles* caught him like a cold,
especially *George Harrison*, who took years to get over it.
Many people parted company with the fab four at this time
thinking they'd gone soft in the head. Whether they had or
not, they all saw sense in the end.

124

MAXI-SKIRTS:
Just as skirts were getting so short that they were turning into belts, there was a sudden reaction from Paris and hemlines plunged to the ankle, where they stayed for many

years. Road accidents declined immediately, but fabric manufacturers breathed a sigh of relief as they went into overtime.

McGOWAN — CATHY:
Buck-toothed star of *Ready-Steady-Go*, an early version of *Top of the Pops*. She spoke with a strong London accent which the powers-that-be obviously thought was cool, and a simpering manner that made your toes curl. Having said that, she became a role model for many late sixties and early seventies teenage girls.

MERSEY SOUND:
This was the term for all the music, good and bad, that came out of Liverpool. The *Beatles*, obviously, were the flagship, but following them came some quite good outfits like *Gerry and the Pacemakers, The Merseybeats* and *The Swinging Blue Jeans* and a few dreadful ones like *Billy J. Kramer and the Dakotas, Freddie and the Dreamers* and the girl

with the voice that sounded like it had been strained through an elephant's trunk — *Cilla Black*. By the time the Beatles split up the whole world was sick to death of the Mersey sound, and Liverpudlians telling us all how bloody fab they all were.

MODS:
A style cult that only happened in Britain, Mods came from nowhere and were totally original. In their tight little bum-freezer Italian suits, fur-trimmed anoraks and pork-pie hats, they cut quite a dash as they zoomed around on their chromed-up Vespa scooters, covered in lights back and front and sporting huge aerials decked with fox tails. Their sworn enemies were the Rockers (see *Rockers*) and a favourite weekend pastime for both cults was to drive down to the seaside and kick the shit out of each other.

MONEY:
In 1971 despite a huge publicity campaign, the whole country was thrown into turmoil when our money went decimal. When your parents make those interminable jokes about things costing half-a-crown, or one-and-sixpence, this is where it comes from. For the last time 10 shillings became 50p, the two-shilling coin became 10p, the one-shilling became 5p. Most of the problems were caused by the poor old people who took years to get used to it.

OP-ART:
A style of painting invented by *Bridget Riley*. It consisted of black and white swirly patterns that made your head ache if you looked at them too long.

OSMONDS:
The term teenybopper was born in 1973. An appalling child group called the *Osmonds* hit England in 1973. Donny and Marie were to make it quite big but the rest of them, including the hideous, podgy nine-year-old Jimmy, sank, thank God, into a well-deserved obscurity. Jimmy's greatest hit was *Long-haired Lover from Liverpool*. Need I say more.

OZ:
A group of hippie Australians led by *Richard Neville* started an underground magazine that was to make history when it was prosecuted for obscenity. Many British artists and writers worked on it (including myself) and never quite knew what all the fuss was about. The trial became a hilarious fiasco and the British legal system and establishment was left, quite rightly, with a great deal of egg on its geriatric face.

PLATFORM SHOES:
Just about one of the ugliest and silliest fashions to arrive in

1972 was platform shoes. Often up to three inches thick, they were responsible for spraining more of your parents' ankles than any sport has ever done. *Elton John*, known for his disastrous fashion sense, spent more time and money on his shoes in those days than he does on his head these days.

POP-ART:

Very much a phenomenon of the late sixties and early seventies. Although originally started by an English painter called *Richard Hamilton* in 1956, it was a brilliant New York screwball called *Andy Warhol* who had the whole art world arguing, in the early sixties, when he produced a huge

OH JULIAN. WHAT A FABULOUS COLLECTION.

painting of a Campbell's soup can. How can this be art, the critics cried? What old Andy was saying, of course, was that everything around us, even the most everyday objects, are just as worthy of having their portraits painted as the usual bowls of fruit or landscapes. At a stroke it punctured all the pomposity regarding figurative art and soon loads of American painters and then later British ones started producing bright, funny, irreverent canvases based on the things they saw around them.

THE PROFUMO AFFAIR:
Your mum and dad will almost certainly remember this
amazing story that stayed on the front pages of every
newspaper throughout and beyond 1963. Two up-market
prostitutes, *Christine Keeler* and *Mandy Rice-Davies*,
managed to get themselves into bed with not only high-up
British politicians including the minister for war *John
Profumo*, but a Russian military attaché (and maybe spy) as
well. This, of course, was definitely not a good thing for
security, and the whole fuss eventually brought the
government down, as John Profumo lied to the House of
Commons (v. serious).

PUNKS:
Everyone knows about punks, but they should be
mentioned purely because of the fuss they caused in the
mid-seventies. If your parents had thumbed their nose at
their parents' generation, the punks simply stuck two
fingers up at theirs. Fashion-wise they were a glorious
disaster area. Ripped bondage clothing, spiked, parrot-
coloured lacquered hair, studs and rings in and around
every orifice, tattoos across foreheads — they simply didn't
give a shit and almost competed with each other to see how
hideous they could look. Brilliant!

RADIO CAROLINE:
The first and most famous pirate radio station started
broadcasting illegally from the North Sea in 1964.
Practically every teenager would tune in to this naughty
non-stop pop music, usually under the blankets late at
night. *Radio Luxembourg* had set the scene for years before
Caroline, but as I said earlier the signal fluctuated so much
that only kids with high-powered radios could listen to it
comfortably. The only credit that you could lay on the

incredibly naff *Tony Blackburn* and *Noel Edmonds* is that they were among those original radio buccaneers.

ROCKERS:
A particularly unsavoury bunch of kids whose watered-down descendants, called bikers, are still around today. Rockers lived for their motorbikes (when the best bikes were British). They were famed for doing the ton (100mph) across red traffic lights and other loony stunts. Their far more disgusting American relatives were (and are still) called Hell's Angels, and I'm sure your stomachs are far too delicate to describe some of the antics they get up to. As described earlier, their enemies were the 'sissy', scooter-driving mods. Many a bike chain would be wrapped around an unsuspecting mod's close-cropped head on their famous days at the seaside.

SIX-FIVE-SPECIAL:
The very first teenagers' music programme, launched in the early sixties. Your mum and dad might just have been allowed to watch it when having their tea on a Friday evening. Unbelievably crudely produced, it's hard to believe it was the direct ancestor of the almost as unsophisticated *Oh Boy, Ready Steady Go* and the over-slick *Top of the Pops*. It was presented by middle-aged-looking personalities like *Muriel Young* and *Pete Murray*. It launched skiffle and a rather weedy British version of rock and roll, but also had soppy balladeers like *Dickie Valentine* and *Craig Douglas*. Needless to say, it was thought to be the hippest thing since sliced bread (for about ten minutes).

SKINHEADS:
Although they looked like a cross-breed of the mods and punks they were around some time before both of them. These lads and ladesses had neither the style of the mods, nor the outrageous humour of the punks, being far more into mindless violence. Number 1 haircuts, all-over tattoos, thick braces holding up short blue jeans and huge Doc Marten steel-capped boots were their stock-in-trade. A group of skin'eads usually shared a single brain cell between the lot of them when they went out looking for trouble. Rare specimens, usually in their late twenties and thirties, can still be seen today. There ought to be a conservation order on the poor dears.

SWINGIN' LONDON:
Never was there a more inflated, over-promoted hype in the history of inflated, over-promoted hypes than Swingin' London. There was a nasty rumour going around (put out mostly by the Tourist Board) in the late sixties that London was 'where it was at'. Anyone who lived through that era spent most of their time looking for it. Mind you, if you call driving up the Kings Road in a purple Mini-Moke covered in pink hearts, wearing a big *Biba* hat and little round sunglasses, listening to the *Mommas and Poppas* swinging, then I take it all back.

TEDDYBOYS:
One of the first postwar cult/fashion movements, the Teds (named after the Edwardians), for a large part of the fifties and early sixties, terrified young kids like your parents with their horrendous gang fights. Dressed in drape, velvet-collared jackets, bright waistcoats, drainpipe trousers, brothel-creepers and bootlace ties, they would tour the streets looking for innocent victims or rival gangs. If they couldn't find anyone to take their maliciousness out on, they would rather stupidly rip up cinema seats. They were devout followers of early American rock-a-billy music and would jive, rather badly, with their pony tailed, skin-tight-jeaned girlfriends in sleazy cafes or coffee bars.

Occasionally, like spotting an osprey, you can see one of these sad creatures, usually in their early fifties, slouching along the street in full kit, almost as menacing as *Cindy's Ken*.

GIMME MORE FROTH OR I'LL SMASH THE PLACE UP

MENU

TROUSER SUITS:
In the early seventies, forecasting the beginning of
'women's lib' it became acceptable for women to wear
trousers at work, which gave birth to the trouser suit.
Fashion gurus thought it would become a national
institution, like the pinstriped suit, but strangely enough,
years later, women decided it was all right to look feminine
and kicked it into touch.

TWIGGY:
A Cockney kid called *Lesley Hornby* shot to fame in 1967
and became just about the most sought-after model that
had ever been. Built like an anorexic stick insect, she
became the role model for every teenager in Britain and

then the world. *Quant, Courrèges* and *Hulaniki* designed almost specifically for girls like her, so heaven help you in 1967 if were short and 'well built'.

TWIST:
Brought from America by *Chubby Checker*, a plump black singer/dancer, the twist blew away every other dance form for nearly a decade. In fact, the concept of dancing without touching your partner was so new that the older generation made a hell of a fuss about it and branded it anti-social. There is a direct, traceable line from the twist to how we dance today.

CARRY ON COPING

So there you have it. Hopefully, I've dealt with most of the major areas that cause friction between you and your parents. And I hope all this helps keep the temperature down. Just remember, you've got to try and convince them that you are aware of all the pitfalls and are willing to discuss them openly — and the best of British luck to you.